THE USBORNE
ILLUSTRATED
CHILDREN'S
BIBLE

Additional design by Nickey Butler

Edited by Jane Chisholm and Georgina Andrews

Digital manipulation by John Russell

This edition published in 2006 by Usborne Publishing Ltd, 83-85 Saffron Hill, London EC1N 8RT, England.
www.usborne.com Copyright © 2006, 2002 Usborne Publishing Ltd. The name Usborne and the devices ⓤ ⓔ are Trade
Marks of Usborne Publishing Ltd. All rights reserved. No part of this publication may be reproduced, stored in a retrieval
system, or transmitted in any form or by any means, electronic, mechanical, photocopying, recording or otherwise, without
the prior permission of the publisher. UE. This edition published in America in 2007. Printed in China.

THE USBORNE
ILLUSTRATED
CHILDREN'S
BIBLE

Illustrated by

Elena Temporin

Retold by Heather Amery

Designed by Laura Fearn

Contents

The Old Testament

The New Testament

THE
OLD
TESTAMENT

The Beginning

Long ago, before there was any time, God created the heavens and
the Earth. At first there was nothing but a vast dark space of
swirling water. God looked at the darkness and made the light.
There was now the light of day and the dark of night. This was
the very first day.

On the second day, God made the sky. He put some of the water in
clouds in the sky, and the rest of the water He made into the seas.
In between the sky and the seas was the air.

Then God collected the seas together so that there was dry land
between them. He ordered all kinds of plants and trees to grow
on the land to produce seeds and fruit. That was the third day.

On the fourth day, God put the brilliant golden sun in the
sky to shine during the day, and the silver moon and
stars to shine at night. Together they marked the
seasons of the year.

Next God created all the fish and creatures that live in
the seas, and all the birds and creatures that fly in the air.
He blessed them, and told them to have their young and to
live all over the earth.

On the sixth day, God made all the creatures that live on the land, from the huge wild animals to the smallest insects that creep among the plants.

Then God picked up a handful of dust, pressed and shaped it. He breathed on it until it became the first living man. He called the man Adam. Because God didn't want Adam to be lonely, he created a woman. He called her Eve.

In those six days God created the whole world and every living thing: all the trees and plants, birds, fish and animals, and the first human beings. He looked at what He had made and saw that it was good.

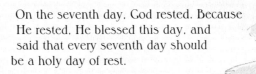

On the seventh day, God rested. Because He rested, He blessed this day, and said that every seventh day should be a holy day of rest.

Adam and Eve

God made a beautiful garden for Adam and Eve, named the
Garden of Eden. He filled it with every kind of flower, and
with trees that had fruit which was good to eat. In the middle
of the garden was the Tree of Knowledge of Good and Evil. He
told Adam and Eve to live in the garden and to look after it. He
said, "You may eat fruit from any of the trees, except fruit from
the Tree of Knowledge. If you eat that, you will die."

Adam and Eve lived very happily in the garden. There were
sparkling rivers of water, and all kinds of birds and animals that
God had made. Adam gave them all names and was friends with
every one. Sometimes, on warm summer evenings, God walked
in the garden with Adam and Eve, and talked to them.

One sleepy afternoon, when Eve was alone, a
snake slithered up to her. "Did God say you
could eat any of the fruit in the garden?" it
whispered in her ear.

"Yes," replied Eve, "we may eat
everything, except the fruit on the Tree
of Knowledge. If we touch or
eat that, we'll die."

"You won't die," whispered
the snake. "God knows that if
you eat the fruit, you'll be wise
like gods and you'll have
knowledge of Good and Evil."

Then the snake slithered away, and Eve
thought about what it had said. At last,
she walked to the Tree of Knowledge in
the middle of the garden. The fruit looked
delicious, and Eve thought she would like
to be wise like a god. Quickly she picked
one of the fruits and took a bite of it.

When Adam came to find her, Eve was
still standing by the Tree, and she gave him
the rest of the fruit. After he had eaten it,
Adam and Eve looked at each other and saw,
for the first time, that they were naked. They
rushed away, and sewed leaves together to
make clothes. When they had dressed in
them, they could look at each
other again.

That evening, God
walked in the garden,
but He could not see Adam
anywhere. "Where are you, Adam?" he called. "I'm here.
I'm hiding because I know now that I'm naked," answered Adam.

"How do you know? Have you eaten the fruit from the Tree of
Knowledge that I told you not to touch?" asked God. "Eve gave it
to me," replied Adam.

"Eve, why did you disobey Me?" asked God. "The snake told me we
wouldn't die if we ate the fruit, but would become wise," said Eve.
"Because you have disobeyed Me, you must leave My garden. You
will have to work hard to grow food. The ground will be rough and
stony. Thorns and thistles will hurt your feet. And when you grow
old, you will die," said God. "If I allowed you to stay, you could eat
the fruit of the Tree of Life, and then you'd live forever. Go now."

Then God drove Adam and Eve out of the Garden.
Dressed in animal skins, they set out, very
miserably, to begin their new, hard life.
God sent an angel with a flaming
sword to guard the Tree of Life,
and angels to guard the Garden
of Eden so that no one could
ever go into it again.

Noah and his Ark

After many, many years, God looked at the world he had created, and regretted what he had done. The people who lived all over the earth had grown very bad; they were cruel to each other, and they no longer listened to God. He decided to destroy the whole world in a huge flood.

There was just one man who loved God and obeyed Him. His name was Noah. God said to Noah, "You must build an ark, a great boat, so that you can save your family and the creatures on the earth from the flood. I will tell you exactly how to build this ark."

Noah listened carefully to God's instructions, and set to work. He cut down trees of the right wood, and collected together all the things he needed. Helped by his three sons, he began to build his ark. First, they marked out the shape of the boat on the ground. Then they made a wooden frame, and covered it with planks of wood. They spread tar on the inside and outside to make it waterproof. After many months of hard work, the ark was finished. It had three decks, a door in the side, and a roof. Noah had built it exactly as God had told him to do. Then Noah and his family collected huge amounts of food and water for themselves and for all the creatures, and spent days loading it onto the ark.

Just as they were checking
that everything was ready, the sky
darkened with huge, black clouds,
blocking out the sun. Then it began to
rain, gently at first, but growing heavier
all the time.

Noah heard a strange noise, getting
louder and louder. He stopped what he was
doing, and looked in the direction of the hills.
A great procession of creatures was coming his
way in an endless line - all barking, mooing,
grunting, whistling and singing. There were two of
every kind of animal and bird in the world.
Noah stared at them, wondering if they
could all fit into his ark. As he watched,
the creatures filed in, and there was just
room for them all. Then Noah and his wife,
his three sons and their wives, went on board,
and when they were inside, God closed the door.

Outside the rain fell steadily for forty days and
nights, and the water slowly covered the ground.
It grew deeper and deeper, until it reached the tops of the
mountains, and everything was drowned in a terrible flood.

14

The ark floated away. For months and months, it was tossed by the waves of this great empty sea. At last, Noah heard the rain stop and the water began to go down a little. He opened a window and sent off a raven. "Go and find some dry land," he said. Away flew the raven but, although it searched for a very long time, it couldn't find any land.

Noah waited for a week or two, and then sent off a dove. The dove flew away but there was still no land for it to settle on, and it returned to the ark. Noah opened the window and let the dove in. Noah waited for another week, and then sent off the dove again. This time it flew back in the evening with an olive leaf in its beak. "That means that the water is going down, and things are growing again," said Noah.

After another week, Noah sent off the dove again but, this time, it didn't come back. Noah lifted the cover off the ark and looked out. He could see that the ark was resting on dry land.

"Noah, you and your family may now leave the ark," said God. "All the creatures are to spread out all over the earth, and have their families. From now on, there will be seasons - summer and winter - to sow the crops and to harvest them."

Noah opened the door, and he and his family rushed out. The sun was shining and the land was dry. The creatures in the ark followed them, and at once started to spread out to repopulate the world. Noah thanked God for saving him, his family, and all the creatures from the flood. In the sky was a rainbow. "That is my sign," said God. "I promise I will never flood the earth like this again."

The Tower of Babel

Long after Noah and his family had left the ark, their children spread out all over the world, and had their own families. They settled where there was good grass and water for their animals, and where they could farm the land. They all spoke the same language, so they could talk and work together.

Some of the people made their way to the east, where they settled on a great plain. There they learned to make bricks of mud and straw, and to bake them hard in the sun. With these bricks, they could build houses to live in.

They were so pleased with their building, they decided to build a city, with a great tower in the middle. The tower would be so high, they thought that it would reach up to Heaven, and all the people would become famous.

God watched the people working on the walls of their city and putting up their tower, brick by brick. He saw they had grown so proud, that they thought they could do anything; they thought they were almost like gods.

Before the tower was finished, God made the people speak in many different languages. Now they could no longer understand each other, or easily work together. Confused, they left the unfinished city, and spread out in all directions, each group speaking their own language. They settled in different places, and grew into great nations in their own countries. The deserted tower became known as the Tower of Babel, after the people who "babbled" in different languages.

Abraham and Sarah

Abraham was a rich farmer who lived with his wife, Sarah, in the city of Haran. They were growing old and, to their great sadness, they had no children.

One day, God said to Abraham, "I want you to leave this city and go to the land of Canaan. I will show you where you are to live, and I will make you the founder of a great nation. I will bless you and you will become famous."

Abraham was a good man, and always did what God told him to do. He prepared for the journey and soon left Haran with his wife, Sarah, his nephew Lot and Lot's wife, his many servants, and his herds of sheep and cows. The journey was long and hard but, at last, they reached the new land, and set up their tents. For a while, they all lived happily together. But as the years passed, the herds of sheep and cows grew bigger and bigger, until there wasn't enough grass and water for them all. Abraham's herdsmen argued with Lot's men about where they should graze their animals.

Abraham decided it was time for he and Lot to separate. He said to Lot, "We mustn't have these arguments. We must part. You choose where you want to live with your family, and your herds." Lot looked at the land. "I'll move down to the valley of the River Jordan where is plenty of lush grass and fresh water," he said.

"Then I'll stay here in the hills," said Abraham, although he knew the grass was thin and dry, and there was little water.

Lot and his wife, his servants, and herds of animals said goodbye to Abraham and Sarah, and made their way east down to the valley. Abraham watched them go. Then God again promised that He would give Abraham all the land he could see, and would make his family into a great nation. Abraham moved to the Plain of Hebron and lived there with Sarah, and his servants, and herds.

One hot afternoon, when Abraham was sitting in the shade, he saw three men crossing the hills, making their way to his tent. Abraham ran out to meet them. "Come to my tent," Abraham said to the strangers. "There you can wash, and rest, and eat with us." Sarah and the servants hurried to get a meal ready. They gave the three men bowls of milk and cheese, made fresh bread, and roasted a calf over the fire. When they had eaten, the men explained why they had come. "We have brought you a message from God," they said. "You and Sarah will have a son."

Sarah laughed. "We are both much too old to have children," she said, but the months went by, and she gave birth to a baby boy. She called him Isaac. She and Abraham were delighted that, at last, they had a child. Abraham also remembered then that God had told him he would be the founder of a great nation.

Isaac and Rebecca

Isaac, the son of Abraham and Sarah, grew up to be a tall and strong young man. Abraham and Sarah were now very old, and Sarah died, leaving Abraham to grieve for her.

Abraham decided that it was time for Isaac to marry, but said his wife had to be from their own people who lived far away from Canaan. Abraham was too old to go on a long journey. He said to one of his servants, "I want you to go to my brother, Nahor, to choose a wife for Isaac."

"What shall I do if she refuses to leave her home? Shall I take Isaac to her?" asked the servant. "No," replied Abraham, "Isaac must stay here in the land that God promised to us. The girl must come here to live with us."

The servant set out on the long journey, taking with him other servants, ten camels, and presents for the girl and her family. When, at last, he reached the city, he stopped at a well outside the walls. It was late in the afternoon, and he knew the women would soon come to the well to fill up their water jugs. But how would he know which of the girls was the right one?

He prayed to God. "Please, God, help me to find a wife for Isaac. I'll say to a girl, 'Please give me a drink of water.' If she says, 'Yes, and I'll also give water to your camels.' then let that girl be the right wife for Isaac."

Almost before the servant had finished his prayer, he looked up, and saw a beautiful girl walking to the well. He watched as she filled her jug at the well, and then asked her for a drink of water. "Yes," she answered, smiling, "and I will give water to your camels." When he had drunk as much as he wanted, the girl filled the jug again and again from the well, and poured it into the trough for the camels.

The servant was delighted because this was the sign he had asked God for. He gave the girl a gold ring and two gold bracelets. "Please tell me who you are, and if there is room in your father's house for me and my companions to stay the night," he said.

"I'm Rebecca, and my grandfather's name is Nahor," answered the girl. "There is plenty of room in my father's house, and there is food and water for your camels." The servant bowed his head, and thanked God for leading him straight to Abraham's family.

Rebecca ran home to tell her family about the man she had met at the well, and showed them the presents he had given her. Rebecca's brother, Laban, hurried back to the well, and asked the servant and the other men to come to his father's house.

After they had fed and watered the camels for the night, the servant, the men, and Rebecca's family washed and sat down to supper. The servant would not start to eat until he had told them why he had come.

He told them about Abraham and Sarah, and about Isaac, their son. He told them how he had prayed to God at the well, and how God had helped him to find the right girl. Then he asked, "Will you allow me to take Rebecca back to Canaan to be Isaac's wife?"

Rebecca's father and her brother, Laban, knew that this was the will of God, and agreed to let her go. The servant said another prayer of thanks to God, and gave presents of jewels to Rebecca and her mother. Then they all had a great feast which went long into the night to celebrate the engagement.

In the morning, Abraham's servant was anxious to leave for home immediately, but Rebecca's family wanted him to stay at least for a few days. "I must go. God has guided me here, and now I must go back to my master," said the servant. "Let's ask Rebecca if she is ready to go," said Rebecca's mother and Laban. Rebecca said that she was willing to leave at once.

The servant and his men loaded up the camels with everything they needed for the long journey. Rebecca said goodbye to her family who gave her their blessing. Taking with her a few maids, Rebecca rode away on a camel to Abraham's family in Canaan.

When, after many days of travel, they at last reached Abraham's tent, it was already evening. Isaac was still out in the fields. He saw them coming and ran to meet them. Rebecca asked who the man was and, hearing that it was Isaac, she got down from her camel. Gazing at the beautiful girl who had come so far to marry him, Isaac hardly heard the servant tell him everything that had happened. He loved Rebecca at once, and soon married her.

The Two Brothers

Isaac and Rebecca lived very happily together, but they didn't have any children. At last, Isaac prayed to God for a son. God heard his prayer and, after some months, Rebecca gave birth to twin sons, whom she called Esau and Jacob. God told her that they would become the founders of warring nations, and that Jacob, the younger of the twins, would rule over his elder brother.

The boys grew up into strong young men. Esau became a hunter who loved to search the hills for wild animals to cook into tasty stews. Jacob preferred to stay near the tents with his mother, Rebecca, who loved him the best of her two sons.

When Isaac was very old, he grew blind. One day, he called Esau to him. "My son," he said, "I'm old, and don't know how much longer I shall live. Go hunting, kill a deer and make it into the tasty venison stew that I enjoy so much. Then I will give you, as my eldest son, my special blessing."

Overhearing Isaac say this to Esau, Rebecca wanted Jacob to have his father's special blessing instead. When Esau went off to hunt in the hills, she told Jacob to bring her two young goats which she would make into a stew. As soon as the stew was cooked, she told Jacob to take it to Isaac, pretending to be Esau.

Jacob did as he was told. He dressed up in some of Esau's clothes, and took the stew and some wine to old, blind Isaac. "Here's your stew, father. I've made it just as you like it," said Jacob. "Is that you, Esau?" asked Isaac. "Yes," lied Jacob. Isaac ate the stew, and then said, "Come here, my son." He prayed to God, and gave his special blessing to Jacob.

When Esau came back from hunting with the meat for the stew,
he soon found that Isaac had already eaten, and had given his
special blessing to Jacob. Esau was so angry, Rebecca was afraid
he would kill Jacob. To save her son, she persuaded Isaac to let
Jacob go to her family where he would be safe, and where he
would find a wife.

Jacob left at once on the long journey north, alone and very
scared. That evening he reached a deserted valley, and lay down to
sleep with only a stone for his pillow. During the night, he dreamed
that he saw a huge ladder reaching up to Heaven. Angels were
climbing up and down it. At the very top was God. God said to
Jacob, "I will give the land you lie on to you and to your family,
which will grow into a great nation. I shall always be with you.
I will look after you, and bring you back to this land."

When Jacob woke up very early the next morning, he was very
frightened, because he felt that God was in this place, and it was
the gate to Heaven. But he remembered what God had said to him,
and he promised that he would always be faithful to God. Then he
went on his journey to find his mother's family.

Jacob and Rachel

Jacob walked alone for many days until, at last, he reached the land where his mother's family lived. He stopped at a well to ask some men with flocks of sheep if they knew his uncle Laban. "Yes," they replied, "and here comes his daughter, Rachel, to water her sheep at the well."

Jacob was overjoyed to meet Rachel. He told her who he was, and helped her to water the sheep. Then she ran home to her father, Laban. When Laban heard that Jacob was at the well, he ran to greet Jacob, and welcome him to his house.

Jacob stayed with Laban and worked for him for a month. Then Laban asked him what he wanted to be paid for his work. "I'll work for you for seven years if you let me marry your younger daughter, Rachel," said Jacob. Laban agreed, and Jacob loved Rachel so much, the seven years seemed to him to pass like seven days.

On the wedding day Jacob longed for, Laban brought his elder daughter, Leah, to marry Jacob. "It's the custom in this country that the younger daughter can't be married before the elder daughter, so you must marry Leah," he said. Leah was a pleasant-looking girl, but it was the beautiful Rachel that Jacob loved.

After the wedding, Laban agreed that Jacob could marry Rachel
as well, but he would have to work for him for another seven years.
Jacob married Rachel; he now had two wives but his house wasn't
a happy one. Jacob loved Rachel more than Leah, which made
Leah unhappy. As the years passed, Leah had six sons and a
daughter, but Rachel had none, which made her unhappy. Then,
at last, she had her first son whom she called Joseph.

During all the years Jacob worked for Laban, his uncle had grown
rich, with huge herds of cows, and flocks of sheep and goats. Now
Jacob longed to go home to Canaan. "Let me take my wives and
children, and go to my own country," he said to Laban. Laban
didn't want Jacob to leave, but he said, "What shall I pay you for
all your work?"

"I don't want money," replied Jacob. "Instead let me take all the
black lambs, and speckled and spotted sheep and goats from your
herds." Laban agreed, and Jacob and his sons sorted out
the sheep and goats. Then Jacob, Leah, Rachel and their
children packed all their possessions on camels and,
taking the sheep and goats, as well as their cows and
donkeys, began their journey.

Jacob sent a message to his brother, Esau, that he was on his way home. Then he heard that Esau was coming to meet him, with four hundred men. Jacob thought that this meant Esau was going to attack and kill him. He prayed to God for help. Then he sent a servant with many of his goats, sheep, camels, cows and donkeys as a present to Esau. The rest of the flocks he sent across a river with his two wives and eleven sons, where he thought they would be safe. Alone and afraid, he waited for Esau.

That night, a man came and fought Jacob. All night they wrestled, without a word being spoken. Jacob didn't know who this stranger was, but he knew he came from God. When the sun rose at dawn, the man said, "Now you must let me go." "I won't let you go until you have given me your blessing," replied Jacob. "What's your name?" asked the man. "It's Jacob," said Jacob. "From now on, your name shall be Israel," said the man. He gave Jacob his blessing, and disappeared.

In the morning light, Jacob saw Esau and all his men approaching in a great cloud of dust. Jacob bowed to his brother and waited, but Esau ran up to him, flung his arms around him and kissed him. "Welcome home, my brother," he said, and they both wept with joy at meeting again. All the old quarrels were forgotten.

Joseph and his Brothers

Jacob settled in Canaan with his two wives, Leah
and Rachel, his eleven sons, and his daughters.
Then Rachel died giving birth to her second son,
named Benjamin. But of all his sons, Jacob
loved Joseph the most, as he was the first son
of Rachel, Jacob's best-loved wife.

Jacob made no secret of his love for Joseph.
He gave the boy a splendid wool coat, in
shades of bright blues, purples and greens.
This made the other brothers jealous, and they
hated Joseph. They hated him even more when
he told them about his dreams. "In my dreams,"
Joseph told them, "you all bowed down to me."
Even Jacob was angry with Joseph for being so
boastful.

One day, Jacob sent Joseph to a distant valley to
check that his brothers and their flocks of sheep and goats
were well. When the brothers saw him coming, one said, "Let's kill
him. We'll tell our father that he was eaten by a wild animal."

"No," said another brother. "We mustn't kill him. Let's put him
in that dry well over there." They stripped off Joseph's coat, and
put him in the pit. Just then, some merchants with camel-loads
of spices passed by on their way to Egypt. The brothers took
Joseph out of the pit and sold him to the merchants for twenty
pieces of silver.

Then they smeared Joseph's coat
with goat's blood, and took it to
their father. "We found this coat, but
don't know who it belongs to," they
said. Jacob at once recognized the coat
and, when he saw the blood, he thought
Joseph was dead. He was heart-broken.

The merchants took Joseph to Egypt and sold him as a slave to
Potiphar, who was the captain of the Pharaoh's guard. Joseph was
alone in a strange land, but he knew God was with him. He worked
hard, and Potiphar was so pleased with him, he put Joseph in
charge of his household. For a while, all went well, but then
Potiphar's wife fell in love with the handsome young man. Because
Joseph remained loyal to Potiphar and refused to love his wife in
return, she began to hate him. She told Potiphar lies about Joseph
and that he had attacked her.

Potiphar was furious. He had Joseph flung into the Pharaoh's
prison. The prison governor liked Joseph and soon put him in
charge of the other prisoners, including some of the Pharaoh's
servants. One had served the Pharaoh his wine, and another had
been the Pharaoh's baker. When they had strange dreams, they
told Joseph about them, and Joseph was able to explain what
their dreams meant. A few days later, just as Joseph had predicted
from the dreams, the Pharaoh had the baker executed, but took the
wine server back into his palace.

Joseph had been in prison for two years when the Pharaoh had a strange dream. He asked his wise men what it meant, but no one could explain it. Then the wine server remembered Joseph. The Pharaoh had Joseph brought from the prison, and the Pharaoh told him his dream.

Joseph listened carefully. Then he said, "Your dream means that for seven years there will be good harvests with plenty of food for everyone. Then there will be seven years of bad harvests when the people will go hungry, and even starve. If you are wise, you will put someone in charge who will store grain from the good harvests, so there is food for the people during the bad ones."

The Pharaoh was so pleased with Joseph, he gave him fine clothes, a gold ring and necklace, and a chariot to ride in. He made Joseph a governor and put him in charge of all the stores of food in Egypt. For seven years, there were good harvests, and Joseph arranged for the surplus grain to be put into safe stores. During the seven years of bad harvests, Joseph had plenty of stored food to sell to the Egyptians and to other people.

The harvests were bad everywhere and, far away in Canaan, Joseph's father, Jacob, and his family were growing short of food. Jacob kept his youngest son, Benjamin, at home, and sent his other ten sons to Egypt to buy grain for bread. "I've heard they have plenty in the storehouses there," he said.

When the brothers reached Egypt, they
went to the governor and asked if they
might buy grain. They bowed in front
of Joseph, but didn't realize that this
man dressed in fine Egyptian clothes
was their brother. Joseph recognized
his brothers immediately. He spoke
to them very sternly. "You're spies
who have come to spy on Egypt," he
accused them. They protested that
this wasn't true, explaining that
they were ten honest brothers, that
they had left one brother at home
with their father in Canaan, and
had another brother who was
dead. They had only come
to buy food, they said.

Joseph had his ten brothers put in prison for three days. Then he released them. "You may go now, but you must leave your brother, Simeon, here in prison and, when you come again, you must bring your brother Benjamin with you." The brothers loaded sacks of grain on their donkeys and began the long journey home. They didn't know that Joseph had secretly put the money they had paid for the grain into the sacks.

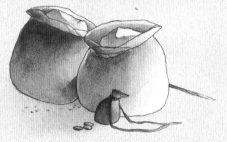

When the nine
brothers stopped to
rest and eat, one of them
found the money in a sack
of grain. They were all very frightened. "God is punishing us for
selling Joseph," they said. They hurried back to their father Jacob,
and told him everything that had happened to them. When Jacob
heard that the governor had kept Simeon, and that the brothers
had to take Benjamin back with them, he was very unhappy.
"Joseph is dead, Simeon is in prison, and now you'll take away
my youngest son, Benjamin. If anything happens to him, I'll die
of grief," he said.

After a while, when all the grain had been eaten, Jacob had to
send his nine sons to Egypt again to buy food. This time they took
Benjamin with them. Again they bowed before the governor and
asked to buy food. They still didn't realize that Joseph was their
brother. Joseph ordered his servants to give them and Simeon a
meal in his house, making sure that Benjamin had plenty to eat.

The next morning, Joseph had the brothers' donkeys loaded with
sacks of grain, and again he had the money they had paid put
back into the sacks. He had one of his silver cups hidden in
Benjamin's sack. The eleven brothers began their journey, but they
hadn't gone far when some of Joseph's guards caught up with
them. They searched the sacks, and found the silver cup in
Benjamin's sack. The brothers were terrified.

The guards marched them back to the governor's house, where Joseph waited for them. They knelt on the ground, and begged for mercy. "You may all go, except Benjamin as the silver cup was in his sack. He must stay here and be my servant," said Joseph.

"Please let us take Benjamin home with us," said Judah, one of the brothers. "Our father has already lost one son. If he loses Benjamin, it will break his heart. Let me stay here instead." Joseph knew then that his brothers had changed, and were sorry for what they had done to him long ago.

"I am Joseph, your brother, whom you sold as a slave," Joseph cried. "God sent me to Egypt, where I am the Pharaoh's governor, to save you from dying of hunger. God promised Abraham that the nation he founded would be safe. Go back to my father, and ask him to come and settle in Egypt. Bring all your wives and children, and all your herds of animals. There will be five more years of bad harvest and hunger, but there is plenty of food here." Then Joseph hugged Benjamin and his other brothers, and wept with joy.

Joseph gave his brothers food for the journey back to Canaan, and new clothes and presents for his father. When Jacob heard that Joseph was alive and well, he was overjoyed and agreed at once to go to Egypt. He and his eleven sons settled there, with all their families. The man from God, who had fought Jacob in the desert long ago, had told him that his name should now be Israel. So Jacob's family in Egypt became known as the children of Israel.

Moses in the Bulrushes

Many years passed, and Jacob's descendants, who were known as
the Hebrews, grew into a large and powerful nation. Joseph lived to
be a very old man. But, after he died, a new, cruel Pharaoh ruled
Egypt. He was afraid that the Hebrews would join forces with
Egypt's enemies and take over the country, so he made them his
slaves. He forced them to work on the land, and to build great
cities and temples. All day they toiled, making bricks of mud and
straw which were baked hard in the hot sun. Guards with whips
watched them, and beat them if they stopped or tried to rest.

Although they were now slaves, the Pharaoh was still frightened of
the Hebrews. He made a new law, and ordered his soldiers to kill
all the Hebrew baby boys as soon as they were born.

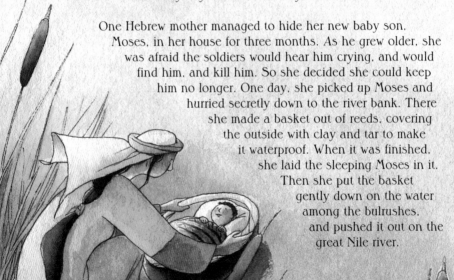

One Hebrew mother managed to hide her new baby son,
Moses, in her house for three months. As he grew older, she
was afraid the soldiers would hear him crying, and would
find him, and kill him. So she decided she could keep
him no longer. One day, she picked up Moses and
hurried secretly down to the river bank. There
she made a basket out of reeds, covering
the outside with clay and tar to make
it waterproof. When it was finished,
she laid the sleeping Moses in it.
Then she put the basket
gently down on the water
among the bulrushes,
and pushed it out on the
great Nile river.

Her young daughter,
Miriam, was hiding in the reeds.
She watched the basket float away down
the river, and followed it, walking along the
river bank to see where it would go. Soon, the
Pharaoh's daughter and her maids came down to bathe in
the river. The Princess noticed the basket floating among the
reeds, and ordered one of her maids to bring it to her.

When the Princess looked at the sleeping baby, she said, "This
must be a Hebrew boy." At that moment, Moses woke up and cried.
The Princess felt so sorry for the tiny baby, she decided to keep him.

Miriam was watching from among the reeds, and she heard what
the Princess said. She ran to her and bowed very low. "Do you
want a Hebrew nurse to take care of the baby?" she asked. "Yes,
bring one to me," ordered the Princess.

Miriam ran to her mother and told her what had happened.
Together they hurried back to the Princess. "Take care of this
baby for me. I'll pay you well," said the Princess.

The mother was delighted to be able to take her baby son home,
knowing that now he was safe. Moses lived with his mother and
the rest of his family until he was old enough to go back to the
Princess. Then his mother took him to the Palace. "He is my
son now," said the Princess, and his mother left Moses to be
brought up as an Egyptian prince.

Moses Saves his People

Moses grew up in the Pharaoh's Palace, and was treated just as if he were an Egyptian prince, but he never forgot he was a Hebrew. It made him very sad and angry to see how cruelly the Egyptians treated the Hebrew people.

One day, he saw an Egyptian slave-driver savagely whipping a Hebrew man. After looking around to make sure that no one was watching, Moses killed the Egyptian and buried his body in the sand. Moses thought he was safe, but someone had seen him. When the Pharaoh heard what Moses had done, he ordered his soldiers to kill Moses.

Hearing that his life was in danger, Moses escaped to the Midian desert. He lived there for a long time, working as a shepherd. One day, he saw a bush that seemed to be on fire, but wasn't burning up. Puzzled, Moses went to look at it.

Then Moses heard a voice. "Do not come any closer, for you are on holy ground." Moses was very frightened. Then the voice spoke again. "I am your God. I am the God of Abraham, Isaac and Jacob. I have seen how cruelly the Hebrews are treated in Egypt. You must go the Pharaoh, and ask him to set them free. Take your brother Aaron with you. The Pharaoh will not agree to let the people go, but I will make him. Then all the world will know that I am God. You will lead the Hebrews to a good land where they will be free, and have plenty to eat."

Moses didn't want to go back to Egypt, but he knew he must obey God. He and Aaron went to the Pharaoh. "The Lord God of Israel says you must let the Hebrews go free," said Aaron.

"I don't know your God. I will not let the people go," answered the Pharaoh. He was so angry, he ordered that the Hebrews were to be made to work even harder than before.

Moses was in despair. He prayed to God for help. "Go to the Pharaoh again, and warn him that if he does not let the people go, I will make terrible things happen in Egypt," answered God.

Moses and Aaron went again to the Pharaoh, but he didn't believe the warning, and again refused to set the Hebrews free. Then the terrible things began. First, the river Nile turned red and stinking, the fish died and no one could drink the water. A week later, thousands of frogs swarmed out of the river, streams and ponds, finding their way into every corner of the Egyptians' houses. Next, clouds of biting flies, then other flies, filled the Pharaoh's palace, and all the houses, except those of the Hebrews. But still the Pharaoh wouldn't let the Hebrews go.

Then the cattle began to die, except in Goshen where the Hebrews lived, and all the Egyptians were ill, with horrible sores on their bodies. After that, there were terrible storms; hail flattened all the crops in the fields, except in Goshen. Next, great swarms of locusts ate everything green that was left. They were followed by three days of total darkness, but still the Pharaoh wouldn't let the Hebrews go.

Then the very worst thing happened. The eldest son of every
Egyptian family died in one night; every son from the Pharaoh's
to the lowest slave. The Hebrews were safe in Goshen because God
had told them what to do. Earlier that evening, each Hebrew family
had killed a lamb, and put a little of its blood on the doorposts of
their house. Then they had roasted the lamb, and eaten it with
herbs and quickly-made flat bread. God said the Hebrews should
always remember the night when death passed over them, and
keep it, every year, as a special feast day, named the Passover.

The Pharaoh sent for Moses and Aaron. "Take your people,
and all your flocks and herds, and go," he said. The
Egyptians were now so frightened by the Hebrews,
they gave them gold, silver, and fine clothes,
and hurried them on their way.

40

The next day, all the Hebrews left Egypt. God led them to the Red Sea with a column of smoke to follow during the day, and a column of fire at night so they could see their way.

Then the Pharaoh changed his mind. He sent his army racing in chariots after the Hebrews. When the Hebrews saw them coming, they were terrified. In front of them was the Red Sea, and behind them were the Pharaoh's soldiers.

Moses told them not to be afraid because God would help them. He pointed across the water, and a strong east wind, sent by God, blew away the water, making a dry path for them to hurry across. When the Egyptian soldiers tried to follow them, the sea rushed back and all the soldiers were drowned.

The Hebrews were free, at last. Miriam played her tambourine, leading the women in a dance for joy. Then they sang to God, praising Him for saving them from the Egyptian army and releasing them from slavery. Now they could travel on to the land which God had promised them.

Moses in the Desert

Moses led the Hebrews to their new land across the desert.
They stopped at wells for water, but they grew hungry, and started
grumbling. They quickly forgot how hard life had been for them
when they were slaves in Egypt. "Do you remember the juicy
melons we had?" said one. "And the onions and cucumbers," said
another. "We always had plenty of bread and meat," said a third.
"It would be better to be slaves in Egypt, than die of starvation in
the desert," they agreed.

God heard the people complaining and said to Moses, "Tell the
people I will not let them go hungry. I will give them meat to eat
every evening, and bread every morning. There will be enough for
each day, but on Fridays, the sixth day, there will be enough for
two days. This is so that on the seventh day, which is the Sabbath,
my holy day, the people will not have to collect food, but will rest."

That evening, flocks of small birds, called quails, landed on the
people's tents and were easy to catch. The Hebrews roasted them
over the fires, and had a good meal. In the morning, the
ground was covered with small white
seeds, so thickly they looked like
frost. People collected the seeds,
ground them into flour, made bread
and baked it. They called it 'manna'
because it was food which came from
Heaven. It tasted like biscuits made with
honey and was delicious.

Every day, the people ate roasted
quail in the evening, and bread made from manna
in the morning. On each sixth day, they did as God had told
them. They collected enough food for two days so that they could
rest on the seventh day.

The people now had plenty to eat, but there was little water in the
hot desert. They started to grumble again. "Did you bring us into
the desert so that we, our children and our flocks and herds would
die of thirst?" they asked Moses.

Moses prayed to God for help. "What shall I do? These people are
almost ready to kill me," he said.

"Take your stick and walk on ahead of the people. Then strike
a rock with it," God said to Moses. Moses did as God told him.
When he struck the rock, a great stream gushed out of it. There
was plenty of fresh water for everyone.

God looked after the people in the desert. Every day He gave them
food and water. He kept his promises to them, so that they would
learn to trust Him.

Moses & the Laws of God

Moses led the Hebrews away from Egypt, across the desert, as God
had told him to do. For months they trekked across the hot,
dry land, but God always sent them food and water. At last, they
stopped and camped at the foot of Mount Sinai. Moses climbed the
mountain to pray to God.

God told him that the people must be ready for Him, that in three
days He would come down the mountain hidden in a cloud, and
would speak to them. The people washed their clothes, and
cleaned the camp ready for the meeting with God.

On the third morning, the sky grew dark, thunder rolled and lightning flashed. The mountain was covered with thick clouds. Smoke and fire gushed out of the top, and the ground shook. They heard the sound of a loud trumpet. The people were terrified; they knew that God was near.

Moses and his brother, Aaron, went up the mountain and God spoke to them out of the fire and smoke. He gave them ten laws that His people must always keep.

God said, "I am your God. You must have no other gods but Me. You must not make idols, nor worship them. When you speak My name, say it with respect. Work for six days and keep the seventh day as a holy day of rest. Always treat your mother and father with respect. Do not kill any human being. Husbands and wives must be faithful to each other. Do not steal. Do not tell lies. Do not be envious of the things others have."

Moses went down the mountain, and told the people the laws God had given them. They agreed to keep the laws and to be God's special people. God had told Moses that He would write down the laws on two blocks of stone, and Moses went up the mountain again to receive them.

Moses was away for so long that first the people grew impatient, and then angry. They said to Aaron, "We don't know what has become of Moses, who led us out of Egypt. Let's make a new god to lead us." Aaron agreed, and collected gold earrings from the people. He melted them down, and made a golden calf, like an Egyptian god. He set it up on an altar, and declared that tomorrow would be a feast day. Next day, the people feasted, danced and sang around the altar, making a great noise. "This is our god who brought us out of Egypt," they said.

God saw how quickly the people had forgotten His laws, and was angry. When Moses came down the mountain with the two blocks of stone on which the laws were written, and saw the golden calf, he was very angry too. He threw down the blocks of stone, and broke them. He smashed the golden calf and the altar. "You have done a terrible thing," he said to the people.

Moses begged God to forgive the people for the wrong they had done. He went up the mountain again, and God gave him two more blocks of stone with the tens laws written on them. Moses carried them down the mountain. This time the people waited for him, and listened when he explained the laws of God to them. They promised to keep them. This made an agreement or 'covenant' between God and his people. Moses led the people on through the desert, but it was many years before they reached Canaan, the land that God had promised them.

The Promised Land

From Mount Sinai, Moses led the people north through the desert in the direction of Canaan, the land that God had promised to give them. Just before they reached Canaan, they camped, and God told Moses to send out twelve men to spy out the land. One man was chosen from each of the twelve tribes, who were descended from Jacob's twelve sons. "Find out what the land is like, and what sort of people live there," Moses told them.

The men went off, and came back after forty days, carrying great loads of grapes, figs and pomegranates. "It is a good land, flowing with milk and honey," they told Moses, "but the people live in huge walled cities. They are like giants; they would crush us as if we were grasshoppers."

When the people heard this, they were in despair. "We should never have left Egypt. It would have been better to die there than die in this desert," they said. Joshua and Caleb, two of the men who had gone to Canaan, tried to encourage them. "Canaan is a good land. God promised it to us. Don't be afraid. He will go with us, and give it to us," they said. But the people wouldn't listen.

God said to the people, "You still haven't learned to trust me. You have forgotten all that I have done for you. Because you don't trust Me, you shall wander through the desert for forty years. Everyone who saw what I did in Egypt will die in the desert, all except Joshua and Caleb. Because they trust Me, they will go and take the land that I promised you."

The people were very unhappy
when they heard that they would
die in the desert, but they still
refused to trust God. Going against
God's orders, some of the men went to
fight the people in Canaan to try to take
over the land, but they were soon defeated.

The years passed and the people grew very tired of living in the
desert. They grumbled about their leaders, and rebelled against
Moses and Aaron. Aaron died and Moses knew he that too had not
much longer to live. He told Joshua, "I'm growing old and I'll never
reach Canaan. You must lead the people there. Don't be afraid; be
brave and strong, for God will be with you."

Then Moses spoke to the people, telling them to obey the laws
of God. He blessed them, and was led by God up Mount Nebo to
the peak of Pisgah. There God showed him the promised land. It
stretched from the cities of Gilead and Dan and the land of Judah,
to the southern city of Jericho, and far away in the west to the sea.

Joshua & the City of Jericho

Moses died within sight of the promised land, and the people mourned for him for many days. Then Joshua took his place as leader, as Moses had said. The time had come at last for them to conquer Canaan. They journeyed on through the desert to the River Jordan, where they camped. On the other side of the river was the promised land.

The river was too deep and wide for them to wade through, but God told them how they should cross it. The priests went in front of the people, carrying a box containing blocks of stone with the laws of God written on them. This box was called the Ark of the Covenant.

The moment the priests stepped into the river, the water stopped flowing, leaving a dry path across the river bed. The priests and all the people crossed safely to the other side. When the last one reached the far bank, the river became a rushing torrent again.

The people camped outside the city of Jericho. It was the time for the Feast of the Passover. The next day, the people made bread from corn they had picked in Canaan. This was the first time they had eaten food which grew in the promised land. Now there was no more manna each morning, for they had left the desert at last.

Joshua looked at
Jericho's enormous stone walls
and huge barred wooden gates. He had a
large army, but there was no way they could break
into the city and capture it. Then God spoke to Joshua.

"The city will be yours, and everything in it. This is what you must
do. For six days you and your men must march in silence around
the city once each day. Seven priests will walk behind you carrying
the Ark of the Covenant. The priests are to carry their trumpets.
On the seventh day, you, your men and the priests are to walk
seven times around the city. Then the priests must blow their
trumpets, and everyone else must shout."

Joshua gave his orders to the people, and they did exactly what
God had told them to do. When the priests blew their trumpets on
the seventh day, Joshua said, "Shout, for God has given you the
city." The people shouted as loudly as they could, and, at that
moment, the city's great stone walls crashed to the ground.

Joshua and his army rushed into Jericho. They killed the people
there and took all the treasure they could find. Then they set fire
to the city. This was the Hebrews' first victory in Canaan, and
Joshua soon became famous. The people settled in the promised
land, where they were also known as Israelites, and all was well for
many years.

Samson, a Mighty Man

Once the Israelites had settled in Canaan, and the years passed, they began to forget their promises to God. They prayed to the gods of those people who lived near them, but still God did not forget them. They had enemies on their borders and often had to fight to protect their land. One very fierce nation, the Philistines, was too strong for them, and ruled over the Israelites for forty years.

One day, God sent an angel to an Israelite named Manoah. Manoah had been married for many years, but his wife hadn't had any children. The angel said to Manoah and his wife, "You will have a son who will save the Israelites from the Philistines." They were amazed to hear this, but delighted to have a son.

When the boy was born, they called him Samson. They let his hair grow long as a sign that he belonged to God in a special way. Samson grew up to be a huge, immensely strong man. One day, when he was walking through a vineyard, a lion roared at him. Samson grabbed the lion and killed it with his bare hands.

Samson knew then that God had given him this great strength for the work he had to do. He fought the Philistines whenever he could. He killed them in battles and set fire to their crops of corn, their vines and olive trees. Soon everyone was talking about Samson. The Philistines tried again and again to trap him.

51

One night, when Samson was in the city of Gaza, the Philistines locked the gates. They thought they had Samson trapped inside and there was no way that he could escape. When it was time for Samson to leave, he went to the gates and lifted them off the gate posts. He carried them away on his shoulders, and dropped them on the top of a hill. The Philistines were furious, and were determined to find a way to kill Samson.

Samson fell in love with a beautiful Philistine girl named Delilah.

The Philistines
thought that they
could use her against
Samson. They promised her
a huge sum of money if she
could discover the secret of
Samson's great strength.

She asked Samson again and again why he was so
strong, but he teased her. "I'll lose my strength if you tie
me up with seven new bow strings," he said, and then,
"Weave my hair into your loom," but, although Delilah tried
these things, Samson remained as strong as ever.

"You would tell me the secret if you really loved me," she said,
when she asked him again. Samson grew tired of the questions
and, at last, he said, "My hair has never been cut. This is a sign
that I belong to God. He gives me my strength."

That night, when Samson was asleep with his head on
Delilah's lap, she quietly called to one of the Philistines
waiting outside. He crept in, she whispered to him what
to do, and the man cut off all Samson's hair. When
Samson woke up in the morning, he was no
stronger than any other man.

With his strength gone, the Philistines
easily overpowered Samson. They put out his
eyes, blinding him; they tied him up in chains, and
dragged him to their city of Gaza. There they put him in prison,
making him work the mill to grind corn into flour. The Philistines
didn't notice that Samson's hair slowly began to grow again.

After many months, the Philistines held a great feast in their
temple dedicated to their god, Dagon. They told the people that
Dagon had helped them capture Samson. As the singing and
dancing in praise of Dagon grew louder and wilder, the people
called for Samson. "Bring him here so we can make fun of him,"
they shouted.

Samson was led from the prison to the temple. He was chained
between two great pillars that held up the roof of the temple,
where the huge crowd of men and women and the Philistines'
leaders could see and laugh at the helpless man.

Samson couldn't see, but he could feel the pillars. He said a silent
prayer to God. "Oh God, give me back my strength just once more.
Let me have my revenge on the Philistines who have blinded me.
Let me die with them."

Samson put his huge hands on the pillars and pushed with all
his might. He pushed the two pillars over, and the whole temple
crashed down, killing the Philistine leaders and thousands of
people. Samson died in this greatest show of his strength, but he
had rescued the Israelites from their hated rulers, the Philistines.

Ruth and Naomi

Elimelech lived in the little town of Bethlehem, in Judah, with his wife, Naomi, and his two sons. There had been bad harvests and everyone was growing hungry. To save his family, Elimelech took them on the long journey across the Jordan River to the country of Moab, where there was plenty of food.

There Elimelech's two sons grew up, and married two girls, named Orpah and Ruth. Then Elimelech died and, later, the two sons also died. Naomi was left alone with her daughters-in-law. When she heard that the crops were good again in Judah and there was plenty of food, she longed to go back to Bethlehem and be with her own people.

"Let us come with you," said Orpah and Ruth, and together the three women left their homes and began the journey back to Judah. They had not gone far when Naomi stopped and said, "You should stay here in your own country and find new husbands." The two girls didn't want Naomi to go on her own, but she insisted. At last, Orpah agreed to stay in Moab and she kissed Naomi goodbye. Ruth begged Naomi, "Please don't make me leave you. I'll go anywhere with you. Your people shall be my people, and your God shall be my God." So Orpah returned to her home, and Naomi and Ruth journeyed on to Bethlehem.

When they reached Bethlehem, it was harvest time for the barley. Naomi and Ruth were very poor. To get food, Ruth walked out to the fields each morning, and picked up the barley the reapers had left behind. She ground it into flour to make bread. She didn't know that the fields belonged to Naomi's rich relation, Boaz.

Boaz saw Ruth in the fields. "Who is that woman?" he asked the reapers. "She came with Naomi from Moab," they said. When Boaz heard how kind Ruth had been to Naomi, he told her she would be safe in his fields, and that she could drink all the water she wanted from his reapers' water jugs.

That evening, Ruth told Naomi what Boaz had said to her. Naomi was pleased because she knew that Boaz was a good, kind man. She also knew that at night Boaz slept near his fields to guard his barley crop from thieves. "After Boaz has had his supper and is asleep, go in quietly, and lie down at his feet," Naomi said to Ruth.

Ruth did as her mother-in-law told her. When she crept in, Boaz heard her. "Who's there?" he asked. "It's Ruth. I've come for your protection," answered Ruth. "There is a man, a close relative of Naomi's, who should look after you and marry you. I'll talk to him tomorrow," said Boaz.

Boaz talked to the man, but the man already had a wife and family, and didn't want to marry Ruth. So Boaz married Ruth, and later they had a son. Naomi was delighted,and very happy that God had given her a grandson.

David and Goliath

Ruth's great grandson, David, worked on his father's farm, looking after the sheep. Although he was only a boy, he was strong and brave. He fought off bears, and even lions, when they tried to steal the sheep. Every day he led the flocks out on the hills, finding the best grass for them. While he watched them, he often played lovely music on his little harp. He also became very good at firing stones with his sling.

One day, David's father asked him to take food to three of his brothers, who were soldiers in the army of King Saul. He was the King of Israel, the kingdom of the Israelites. For many years, the Israelites had been fighting the Philistines. Now King Saul's army was camped on one side of the valley. On the other side was the Philistine army. The two armies watched each other, neither daring to attack.

One Philistine soldier was a giant of a man whose name was Goliath. He was immensely strong, and wore a huge breastplate, and carried an enormous shield and a spear. Every day, he shouted across the valley to King Saul. "Send one of your men to fight me. Whoever wins the battle, wins for the whole army. The losers will become servants of the victor."

The soldiers in King Saul's army listened to the challenge, but none of them dared to go. When David reached the camp and was talking to his brothers, he heard Goliath shouting across the valley. He went to King Saul. "I'll go and fight him," he said.

"You can't go. You are only a boy, and that man is a trained soldier," said King Saul. "I'm not afraid. When I was looking after my father's sheep, I killed bears and lions. God saved me from them, and he will save me from Goliath," replied David.

"You may go, and may God go with you," said King Saul. "But you must wear my fighting clothes, and take my sword." David put on a helmet and a coat of chain mail, and picked up a sword. But they were so heavy he could hardly walk, so he took them off again. "I can't wear them," he said.

He picked up his shepherd's stick and chose five small stones from the bed of the stream. He put them in a bag, took his sling, and strode down the valley to meet Goliath.

When Goliath saw David coming, he laughed. "Are you the champion? Come here, boy, and I'll kill you," he shouted. David walked on. "You have a sword, shield and a spear, but I have God to help me," said David. He put one of the little stones in his sling, swung the sling around and around his head, and let the stone fly. The stone shot straight at Goliath, and hit the giant right in the middle of his forehead. Goliath fell down on the ground. David ran up to him and saw that he was dead. He had killed the Philistine.

When the Philistine army
saw their champion lying
dead on the ground,
they were so frightened
they all ran away. King
Saul's army chased
them, right up to the
gates of their city.
With God's help,
David had won a
great victory for
the Israelites over
the Philistines.

David the King

David's great victory over Goliath made
him famous, and King Saul was so
pleased, he ordered David to stay
with him. There David met King
Saul's son, Jonathan, and he
and David instantly became
the greatest of friends.
They loved each
other as if they
were brothers.
Jonathan gave David
his cloak and a sword.
They vowed they would
be friends forever.

King Saul put David in charge of
his army, and told him he could marry his
daughter, Merab. David soon became a great soldier and
was very popular. Everywhere he went, people sang his praises.
But King Saul soon became jealous of him, fearing he wanted to
be king in his place. So King Saul made Merab marry another
man, but when he saw that David loved his other daughter, Michal,
he made a plan. "You may marry Michal," he said, "but first you
must kill a hundred Philistines." King Saul was sure David would
be killed in the battle, but David fought the Philistines and killed
two hundred of them. Then he married Michal, but all was not well.

Jonathan warned David that
King Saul wanted to kill him.
He begged his father to save
David, and King Saul promised that
he would, but he soon changed his mind.
One evening, when David was playing his harp to
King Saul, the King hurled a spear at him. It whistled past
David and stuck into the wall, just by his head. David knew then
that his life was in danger.

That night, King Saul ordered
his guards to watch David's house
and to kill him in the morning.
David and Jonathan sadly said
goodbye to each other and swore
they would always be friends.
Michal helped David to climb out
of a window and slide down a rope
to avoid the guards. David escaped
in the dark to the hills where he
lived as an outlaw with a band of
men. They fought many battles with
the Philistines, but constantly had to
move their camp around the country
because King Saul had sent his
army to find and kill David.

When King Saul's army was getting very close, David and his men pretended to be on the side of the Philistines, and stayed in their town of Ziklag where they were safe. The Philistines marched out to fight King Saul's army, and David and his men went with them. There was a terrible battle on the mountains of Gilboa, and Jonathan and King Saul's other sons were killed. King Saul was so badly wounded that, rather than be taken prisoner by the Philistines, he killed himself.

When David heard that Jonathan was dead, he wept with sorrow, and mourned for his beloved friend. He cried a great lament: "Saul and Jonathan were lovely and much loved in their lives. In death they were still together. They were swifter than eagles and stronger than lions. How the mighty have fallen in battle."

David went to Hebron where he was crowned king of Israel, but he had to fight many battles against King Saul's followers and against the Philistines. Then he marched to Jerusalem and captured the city from a tribe of Canaanites. He made it his capital, and had the Ark of the Covenant, the box containing the blocks of stone on which God had written the laws, brought there. When it arrived, there was a huge celebration, with singing, dancing and feasting.

David was a good king, a brave soldier, and a great leader, and he was loved by his people. He had many sons and daughters, and always remained faithful to God.

For many years, all went well, until one of David's sons, Absalom, wanted to be king. He gathered an army and fought with David's army, but David's army won. Absolom tried to escape on a mule, but was caught in the low branches of a tree. David's men found him hanging there and, against David's orders, killed him. So, instead of celebrating his victory, David deeply mourned the death of his son.

Over the years of peace that followed, David grew old and tired, and there was trouble about who should be king after him. Before he died, David called for Zadok the priest and said, "My son Solomon is to be king when I die. Take him to the spring at Gihon and annoint him king." The people there brought Solomon back to Jerusalem, shouting with joy. David told Solomon, "Obey God and keep his commands. If you do, He will keep His promise to me that my descendants will always rule this nation." Later, David died and Solomon became King of Israel.

Solomon the Wise

David's son, Solomon ruled
the kingdom of Israel and
lived in the great city of
Jerusalem. One night,
Solomon dreamed that
God came to him and
asked, "What would you
like Me to give you?"
Solomon answered, "I'm
very young to be a ruler
and know I have much to
learn. I would like You to make
me wise so that I can rule your
people justly and well."

God was pleased with Solomon's request. "You could
have asked to be very rich and famous, and for the death of
all your enemies," said God. "As you have asked only for wisdom,
I will make you the wisest man in the whole world. I will also make
you rich and famous, and you will live until you are very old."
King Solomon soon became well-known for his wise judgements,
and people came to listen to the many wise things he had to say.
But he always remembered that his wisdom came from God.

One day two women, one carrying a baby, came to his court to ask
for his judgement. The first woman said; "This woman and I live in
the same house. A few days ago, we both gave birth to babies.
This woman's baby died, but she stole my baby during the night,
and put her dead baby in my son's place. Now she claims that this
baby is hers."

64

"No, your baby died. This baby is mine. I know he is my child," screamed the second woman. "Bring me my sword," King Solomon ordered one his guards. When the sword was brought, King Solomon said, "Now, cut the baby in half, and give half to each of these women." The second woman shouted, "Yes, kill the baby, then neither of us can have him." But the first woman begged, "My lord, please don't kill this child. Give it to this woman so that he may live." King Solomon knew then that this was really the mother, as she would rather give up her child than see him die.

"Give this woman the baby," he ordered, and he sent the two women away. When all the people in Israel heard of this judgement, they knew that King Solomon's wisdom came from God.

Solomon and his Temple

Solomon had been King of Israel for four years when he began his plans to build a House of God, a Temple, in the city of Jerusalem. He sent hundreds of men to the hills to dig out stone from the quarries, and to cut it to exactly the right size and shape for the foundations. Solomon wanted cedar wood to line the walls of the Temple. The best cedar trees grew to the north where the land was ruled by King Hiram of Tyre.

King Solomon made a treaty with King Hiram. Hiram agreed to have the trees felled and floated in rafts down the coast to the Temple. In return, Solomon agreed to send huge amounts of wheat and oil to Hiram every year.

Thousands of men worked on the Temple. There were two rooms. The inside room was square with no windows. Two huge beasts, carved of olive wood and covered with gold, stretched out their wings over it. This was the most holy part of the Temple. Only the high priest went into it on one day of the year. This was at the time of the special feast, known as the Day of Atonement.

In the outer room was an altar and ten lamp stands. The walls were lined with cedar wood, and carved with flowers, trees, and creatures with wings. Everything, including the wooden floor, was covered with gold. At the entrance to the Temple were two bronze pillars, and on the backs of twelve bronze oxen was a huge basin. Outside the Temple were courtyards where the people could come to say their prayers to God.

After seven years, the Temple was finished at last. Solomon had
made it as beautiful as he could, and he filled it with treasure. He
called all the priests and the people to a great and very solemn
ceremony. The priests put the Ark of the Covenant into the sacred
inner room, and the presence of God filled the whole Temple.

Outside, King Solomon stood in front of the people, and prayed to
God. "Oh Lord God of Israel, there is no other God like You, who
loves His people and keeps His promises to them. Watch over Your
Temple, hear the prayers of Your people, forgive them when they do
wrong, and help those who love You and obey You." Then
Solomon turned to the people and said, "May God always be with
us. May we always be true to Him, and obey his commands."

When the ceremony was over, King Solomon gave a great feast for
the people, which lasted for seven days. Then he blessed them,
and they went home, happy and grateful for all that God had done
for the people of Israel.

Elijah

King Solomon's reign was a long and glorious one. Merchants brought rich cargoes to Israel, and Solomon built fine buildings and fortresses. He married many foreign princesses, who brought their own gods with them. When Solomon was old, he forgot his promises to God, and was persuaded by his wives to worship their gods. God warned Solomon to keep His commands, but Solomon took no notice. At last, God said, "Because you have not remained faithful to Me, your son will lose most of your kingdom."

After Solomon died, his son Rehoboam became king, but the kingdom of Israel split into two parts. Judah, the southern part, which included the city of Jerusalem, was loyal to King Rehoboam. But the ten tribes in the northern part chose Jeroboam, who had been one of Solomon's officials, to be their king. Jeroboam made two golden bulls. He wanted his people to worship them as gods instead of going to the Temple in Jerusalem.

After Jeroboam died, many kings ruled the northern kingdom of Israel. The seventh king, Ahab, built a temple for Baal, one of the gods of his people and his wife, Jezebel. Queen Jezebel was very cruel and killed many of the people who were faithful to God. One brave man, Elijah, still loved and obeyed God. He warned King Ahab that there would be no rain for many years and the people would starve.

To keep Elijah safe, God said to him, "Go to the Kerith valley and live there. You can drink water from the stream, and ravens will bring you food."

Elijah did as God told him. Every morning
and evening, ravens brought him bread and meat, and
he drank water from the stream. After a while, as there was no
more rain, the stream dried up. God then told Elijah to go near the
city of Sidon, where a poor widow would give him food.

When he reached the place, Elijah met a widow picking up a few
sticks for her fire. "Please give me a drink of water and some
bread," Elijah said to her. "I have no food," replied the woman. "All
I have is a little flour and a few drops of olive oil. I'm going to bake
one last loaf of bread over a fire made from these sticks. Soon,
when my son and I have finished the loaf, we will starve to death."

"Go home," said Elijah, "and bake a small loaf of bread for me, and
one for you and your son. God says that, from now on, you'll find
that your flour and oil will never run out until the rains come
again." The woman did as Elijah told her, and found that every day
she had just enough flour and oil to make bread for her son,
herself, and for Elijah.

But, one day, the woman's son became very ill, and soon died. The
woman was heartbroken. "Why have you done this to me? Is it to
punish me? Have you told God of all the wrong things I have done
in my life?" she cried. "Give the boy to me," said Elijah. He carried
the boy upstairs to his room and laid him on his bed. Then Elijah
prayed three times to God, "O Lord my God, why have You brought
misery to this woman who has been kind to me? Please bring this
boy back to life."

God heard Elijah's
prayer and answered it.
The boy sat up, alive
and well. Elijah picked
him up and carried him
downstairs to his mother.
"Look," he said, "your
son is alive." The woman
was overjoyed. She took
the boy in her arms and
said, "I know now that
you really are a man of
God, and what you
say is true."

There was no rain for three years. Nothing grew and the people
were starving. Elijah went to King Ahab and told him that he had
brought terrible trouble to Israel by praying to the god Baal.
Elijah said that the priests of Baal and the people
should meet him on Mount Carmel.
King Ahab agreed.

When all the
priests and the
people arrived at
Mount Carmel,
Elijah said, "You
can't worship Baal and
God. Let's see which is
the true God." Then he said
to the priests of Baal, "Build an
altar to Baal, and I'll build one to God.
The god which lights the fire on the altar
is the true god."

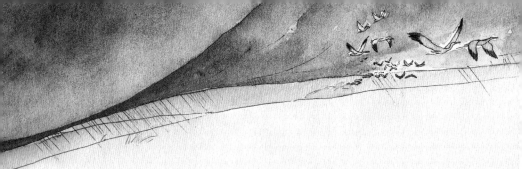

The priests built the altar and laid wood on it. Then they prayed to Baal to set fire to the wood. All day they prayed, but nothing happened. Elijah built his altar and piled wood on it. He poured water over the wood, soaking it. Then he prayed, "O Lord God of Israel, let the people see that You are God, and return to You."

At once, God sent down fire, setting alight the wood, which burned fiercely. The people watched, and then flung themselves down on the ground. "The Lord, He is God," they shouted.

Elijah walked up to the top of Mount Carmel and prayed to God for rain. After a while, the sky grew dark with great, massed clouds, and the rain began to lash down. Elijah was overjoyed. He was so excited, he tucked his cloak into his belt, and ran in front of King Ahab's chariot all the way to Jezreel, in the kingdom of Judah.

The next day, everything changed. Queen Jezebel wanted Elijah killed and he had to run for his life. He ran on and on until he came to the desert, and then to Mount Sinai. There he was alone. "Elijah, why are you here?" Elijah heard God ask him. "They have killed all Your prophets, and they want to kill me," answered Elijah. "Go back. Go and find Elisha, who will be My prophet after you. There are still thousands of people in Israel who have stayed faithful to Me. And remember that I am with you," said God.

Elijah did as God told him. He found Elisha at work in the fields. Elijah took off his cloak, and put it around Elisha's shoulders to show that he was to be the next prophet in Israel. Elisha left home and went with Elijah on his journeys around the country, teaching the people about God.

Naboth and his Vineyard

King Ahab lived in Jezreel. Next to his palace was a vineyard which belonged to a man named Naboth. King Ahab wanted the vineyard for a garden. "Sell me your vineyard, or exchange it for an even better one," he ordered Naboth.

Naboth refused. "The vineyard belongs to my family, and I want to leave it to my son. It would be against God's laws to sell it." King Ahab was very angry. When Queen Jezebel asked, "What's troubling you?" King Ahab told her about the vineyard. "Aren't you King of Israel? You shall have your vineyard," she said.

Queen Jezebel had Naboth falsely accused of going against God's laws, and of treason against the King. He was convicted and stoned to death. The Queen then told King Ahab that Naboth was dead, and he could have the vineyard.

King Ahab went to the vineyard but found that God had sent Elijah there to meet him. "God says you have caused the death of an innocent man. For that, you will die," said Elijah. "Queen Jezebel will die here in Jezreel, and your whole family will be wiped out."

King Ahab was horrified. He changed his ways, and God saw that Ahab was ashamed of what he had done. For a while, there was peace in Israel. After three years, King Ahab joined forces with King Jehoshaphat of Judah, and they went to war against the Syrians. There was a terrible battle. King Ahab was shot by a bowman and died of his wounds. Later, Queen Jezebel was killed in Jezreel. Elijah's words had come true.

Elisha and Naaman

Elijah was growing old, and knew he had not long to live. Elisha
went with him on his last journey. When they had crossed the
Jordan River, Elijah said, "I shall leave you soon. What would you
like me to give you?" Elisha replied, "I'll carry on your work alone.
Leave me your power." "That is a hard thing to do, but if you see
me when I go, then you will know that you've been given what you
asked for," said Elijah.

At that moment, a fiery chariot drawn by fiery horses swept
between them. There was a great gust of wind, and Elisha saw
Elijah being taken up to Heaven. Elisha knew then that he had
been given the power he had asked Elijah for. Sadly, he picked up
Elijah's cloak which had fallen to the ground, and went away to
continue Elijah's work.

Naaman was the commander of the Syrian army. He was a brave
soldier and a rich man with a big house and lots of servants,
but he had a horrible skin disease, called leprosy.
Naaman's wife had a new slave, a young girl
who had been captured by the Syrians
during a raid on Israel. She said to
Naaman's wife, "If Lord Naaman
would go to the prophet Elisha
in Israel, I know he would be
cured of his disease."

When his wife told Naaman what the girl had said, he asked the King of Syria for permission to go to Israel. The King gave him a letter for the King of Israel so that Naaman could travel safely through the country.

Naaman rode off in his chariot with many servants, and lots of money and clothes. When he reached Elisha's house, a servant came to the door. "My master says you must go to the Jordan, and wash seven times in the river. Then you will be cured," said the servant. Naaman was furious. "Why won't Elisha come to see me?" he shouted. "I thought he'd call on his God and I would be cured. Why must I wash in the Jordan? There are better rivers in Syria."

Angrily, he started to drive away in his chariot, but one of his servants stopped him. "My master," said the servant, "if Elisha had asked you to do something difficult, you would have done it. As he only says you should wash in the Jordan, shouldn't you try it?" Naaman realized that the servant was right. He drove to the Jordan and washed in it seven times. When he walked out of the river, his skin was clear and smooth. He was cured of the disease.

Delighted, Naaman rushed back to Elisha to thank him. "I know now that there is only one true God," he said. He tried to give Elisha all the gifts he had brought with him, but Elisha wouldn't take them. He blessed Naaman and sent him home. Elisha did many wonderful things. He knew that God always protected him, and he became so famous that kings asked his advice, but he was always ready to help anyone in trouble. When Elisha died, all the people in Israel mourned him.

Jeremiah

Jeremiah lived in Judah. He was called by God to be His prophet. God told him that he must warn the people of Judah that terrible things would happen to them unless they gave up praying to the false gods and became faithful to the one true God. Jeremiah was afraid. "Lord God," he said, "I'm too young to do this and I'm no good at speaking in public." God replied, "I chose you before you were born. I will tell you what to say, and I will always keep you safe."

The little kingdom of Judah was ruled by King Josiah, but there was always war with his enemies on his borders. Josiah was killed fighting the Egyptians who were marching north through his land to join the Assyrians in battle against the Babylonians.

Over the years, Jeremiah told the people in Judah again and again what God told him to say, but they took no notice. One day, he went to a potter and watched him shape a clay pot on his wheel. When the pot became lopsided, the potter squashed the clay into a lump, and began to make the pot again.

God said to Jeremiah, "The people of Israel are like clay in My hands. I can destroy them if they persist in doing evil, but I can remake them if they change their ways." Jeremiah told the people what God had said to him, but still they wouldn't listen.

Another time, Jeremiah stood in front of the Temple in Jerusalem. He shouted to the people. "God says if you won't listen to Him and obey His laws, He will destroy the Temple and the city of Jerusalem." The priests in the Temple were so angry with Jeremiah, they had him beaten and put in prison.

Jeremiah couldn't speak to the people then, but he could write to them. He spent many hours writing to the King of Judah, but the King threw the parchment on the fire. So Jeremiah wrote it all out again, but it was no use.

Nebuchadnezzar, the King of the Babylonians, led his army to Jerusalem. He made Zedekiah King of Judah, and took thousands of people prisoner, marching them back to Babylon to work as slaves. Zedekiah ruled Judah for ten years, and then he rebelled against the Babylonians. Nebuchadnezzar led his army again to beseige Jerusalem.

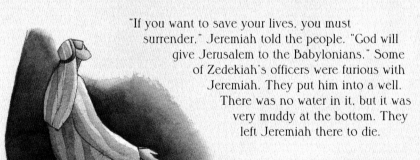

"If you want to save your lives, you must surrender," Jeremiah told the people. "God will give Jerusalem to the Babylonians." Some of Zedekiah's officers were furious with Jeremiah. They put him into a well. There was no water in it, but it was very muddy at the bottom. They left Jeremiah there to die.

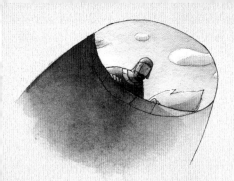

A man named Ebedmelech, who worked in the King's palace,
asked for permission to rescue Jeremiah. The King agreed, and
Ebedmelech and some men let down ropes into the well, and
pulled Jeremiah to safety.

King Zedekiah asked Jeremiah what he should do. "You must
surrender, or Jerusalem will be destroyed," answered Jeremiah.
Zedekiah refused, and tried to escape from the beseiged city. He
was captured by the Babylonians, who blinded him, and killed his
two sons. Then he was led in chains to Babylon.

Nebuchadnezzar's army broke through the walls of Jerusalem.
They destroyed the King's palace, smashed the Temple and the
houses, and set fire to them. They carried away all the treasure
from the Temple, and marched thousands more Israelites in chains
back to Babylon.

Jeremiah stayed with the few people who were left. The people of
Judah hadn't listened to God's warnings, and now they had been
punished. Jeremiah wrote to the people who were living in exile in
Babylon. "God says," he wrote, "He promises that one day He will
bring you home. While you are in exile, you will learn to love Him
again. You will remember His laws and do what is right. Look
forward to the time when you will return to your own land."

The Story of Daniel

Daniel was one of the many Israelites who were captured by King Nebuchadnezzar's army and taken from Jerusalem to the far-off city of Babylon. There, together with other good-looking, intelligent boys from some of the best families, he was selected for special training. King Nebuchadnezzar ordered that the boys should be well taken care of, taught the Babylonians' language, study their writings, and learn from their wisest men. He had food sent to them from his own kitchens.

Daniel and three of his friends, Shadrach, Meshach and Abednego, wanted to keep God's laws about what they should eat, so they refused to eat the King's food. "Let us eat only vegetables and drink water," Daniel said to the court official in charge of them. "My life will be in danger if you get thinner than the other boys, or get ill," said the official, who had grown fond of Daniel. "But you may try it for ten days."

After the ten days, Daniel and his friends were in better health than the other boys, and they were very good at their lessons, so they were allowed to eat their own food. The years passed, and Daniel grew as knowledgeable and wise as the wise men in Babylon. He was also good at understanding what dreams meant. The King was so pleased with Daniel and his friends, that he made them officials in his court.

One night, King Nebuchadnezzar had a frightening dream which terrified him. In the morning, he sent for all his wise men. "I had a dream last night, but now I can't remember what it was. You must tell me what it was and what it means," he ordered. "We could say what it meant if you would first tell us what your dream was," answered the wise men.

"*You* must tell me my dream," shouted the King. "No one on earth
can tell you that," replied the wise men. The King was furious.
He ordered all the wise men in Babylon to be killed.

When his soldiers went to arrest Daniel, he said, "Let me speak
to the King. I'll tell him about his dream." Daniel and his friends
prayed to God for His help, and to save them from being killed with
the wise men. That night, Daniel dreamed that God told him what
the King's dream meant.

The next day, he was taken to the King. "Sire," he said, "you
dreamed that you saw a gigantic statue with a head of gold,
a body of silver and bronze, legs of iron, and feet of iron and clay.
Suddenly, a stone shattered the feet, and the whole statue came
crashing down to the ground. It broke into tiny pieces of dust
which were blown away by the wind. Then the stone became a
huge mountain which covered the whole earth."

"I'll tell you what this dream means," continued Daniel. "The
golden head of the statue is you, great King. The silver, bronze,
iron and clay are the empires which will come after yours. Some
will be strong, some will be weak, but none will last forever. The
stone which broke the statue is the Kingdom of God, which will
never be destroyed."

King Nebuchadnezzar was very impressed by what Daniel told him.
"Your God is the God of gods, if he can reveal such mysteries to
you," he said. He gave Daniel many gifts, and appointed him
governor of all Babylon, and the chief of all his wise men. At
Daniel's request, the King also gave important positions to
Daniel's three friends, Shadrach, Meshach, and Abednego.

Some years later, King Nebuchadnezzar had a huge golden statue, nearly ninety feet high, made of one of his gods. He had it set up on the Plain of Dura, and ordered all his governors, officers, judges and advisors to attend a great ceremony of dedication. Musicians were there to play pipes, lyres and harps. But Daniel had stayed behind in the palace in Babylon.

"When you hear the music," ordered the King, "you are all to bow down and worship the god, or you'll be burned to death in a furnace."

Everyone there did as King Nebuchadnezzar ordered, except Daniel's three friends, Shadrach, Meshach, and Abednego. When the King heard that they had refused to worship the god, he was furious, and told them they would die.

"Our God can save us from the fire," they said. "But even if He doesn't, we won't worship any other god. We won't bow down to the statue."

In a rage, the King ordered the fire in the furnace to be made seven times hotter than usual. Then the three friends were tied up and thrown, fully clothed, into it. As the King watched, they walked unharmed through the flames and, suddenly, there was a fourth man with them. The King was astonished. He stared and stared. "I can see four men, and the fourth one looks like a god," he said.

The King walked to the furnace. "Shadrach, Meshach and Abednego, come out," he called. The three friends stepped out. Everyone saw that they were no longer tied up, and there wasn't a mark of burning on their clothes or hair. They didn't even smell of smoke.

"Blessed be the God of these men, who sent an angel to rescue them. I order that no one shall say a word against their God, or against these men," said King Nebuchadnezzar. He then promoted the three friends to positions of power in Babylon.

Belshazzar's Feast

Daniel lived on in Babylon and, later, King Nebuchadnezzar died and his son, Belshazzar, became King. One day King Belshazzar gave a great feast for a thousand of his lords. To show off his riches, he ordered his servants to bring him the gold and silver cups that his father had stolen from the Temple in Jerusalem.

King Belshazzar told his servants to fill the cups with wine, and he, and his lords and wives drank, toasting their own gods. They were all laughing and shouting when, suddenly, they saw a human hand writing on a wall. They watched in silence, and the King was so frightened that his knees shook.

"Call all my wise men," he croaked. When they came, he said, "The man who can tell me what these words mean shall be the third ruler of my kingdom." But none of the wise men could explain them.

Then the Queen remembered that Daniel had told the King what his dream meant. Daniel was summoned to the King. "Tell me what this means, and I'll make you rich and powerful," said the King.

Daniel looked at the writing. Then he said, "You have shown disrespect to God by drinking to your gods from the cups taken from His Temple. Your kingdom will be divided between the Medes and the Persians." That night, Daniel's warning came true. The Medes and Persians captured the kingdom, Belshazzar was killed, and Darius of the Medes was made King of Babylon.

Daniel and the Lions

Daniel was growing old, but King Darius thought Daniel was so wise, that he appointed him to be one of the three rulers of Babylon. They ruled the kingdom under the king. Daniel served the King loyally, but he still prayed to God. Three times every day, he knelt at his window, facing distant Jerusalem, to say his prayers.

The other two rulers of the kingdom were jealous of Daniel, and plotted to get rid of him. But however hard they tried, they couldn't find anything they could accuse him of doing wrong. They decided that the only way was through his devotion to God.

They went to King Darius and begged him to make a new law. "O King," they said, "make a law that for thirty days everyone must pray only to you. If anyone prays to any other god, they shall be fed to the lions." The King agreed and made the law that could never be changed.

Daniel heard about the new law, but three times every day he knelt at his window to say his prayers to God. The two rulers watched him and, delighted that their plan had worked, they rushed to tell the King.

King Darius was angry and upset. He liked and trusted Daniel, but Daniel had broken the law, and must die. There was nothing the King could do to save him. He ordered Daniel to be put into the lion pit. As Daniel walked down into it, a huge stone was pushed across the entrance to close it. King Darius said, "May the God you trust in save you."

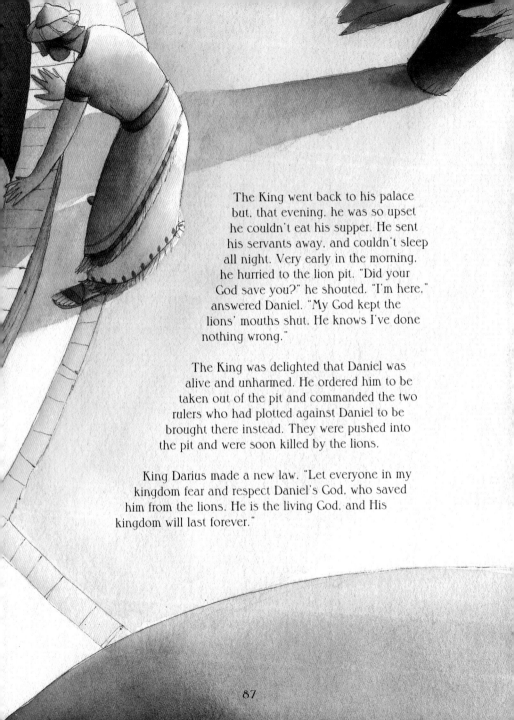

The King went back to his palace but, that evening, he was so upset he couldn't eat his supper. He sent his servants away, and couldn't sleep all night. Very early in the morning, he hurried to the lion pit. "Did your God save you?" he shouted. "I'm here," answered Daniel. "My God kept the lions' mouths shut. He knows I've done nothing wrong."

The King was delighted that Daniel was alive and unharmed. He ordered him to be taken out of the pit and commanded the two rulers who had plotted against Daniel to be brought there instead. They were pushed into the pit and were soon killed by the lions.

King Darius made a new law. "Let everyone in my kingdom fear and respect Daniel's God, who saved him from the lions. He is the living God, and His kingdom will last forever."

Home to Jerusalem

Cyrus, who ruled Persia from his palace in Babylon, was a good king. He put out a proclamation, saying: "The Lord God of Israel has told me to build a house for Him in Jerusalem. All his people are free to go home to rebuild the Temple that Solomon built. I will return all the treasures that King Nebuchadnezzar stole from the Temple before he destroyed it."

The Israelites, or Jews, as they were also known, were overjoyed that they were free to go home at last. In all, forty-two thousand people prepared for the journey across the desert. They took with them their servants, and horses, mules and camels, all loaded with goods and food. When they reached Jerusalem, they began work to rebuild the Temple at once. Many people gave gifts of gold and silver to pay for the stone masons and carpenters, and provided them with food. First the workman laid the foundations of the Temple. When they were finished, the priests sang songs of thanks and praises to God.

The people who had had been living in Judah while the Jews were in exile in Babylon offered to help with the building work. But the Jews refused; they wanted to do it all themselves. This led to trouble with the people living there, and work on the Temple stopped for a long time. Instead, the Jews worked on their houses until some of God's prophets made them feel ashamed. "God's house is in ruins while you work on your own houses," they said.

So the Jews returned to work on the Temple, until it was finished. It was not as impressive as the great Temple built by King

Solomon. but it was a very splendid building. The priests held the Feast of the Passover there and the people celebrated with great joy. giving thanks to God.

The years passed and the Jews lived peacefully in Jerusalem. Back in Babylon was a scholar. named Ezra. who had stayed in Persia. He studied the Laws given by God to Moses. and he felt that the Jews in Israel didn't know God's Laws. He went to the King and asked for permission to go to Jerusalem to teach the people there.

"You may go." said the King. "and anyone who wants to may go with you. I'll give you gold and silver. and other things you need for the Temple of God." So Ezra left Babylon with many of the other Jews who had stayed in the city. The journey was long and dangerous. but God kept them from harm as Ezra knew He would. and they reached Jerusalem safely.

There Ezra found that not all the people were keeping to God's Laws. Some of the Jewish men had married foreign wives who had brought their own gods with them. This was what had led to the destruction of Jerusalem. when the people were taken into exile. all those years ago.

Ezra called all the people in Judah to come to Jerusalem in three days' time. When they had gathered in front of the Temple. he said. "You have broken your promises to God." Then he taught them God's Laws and how they should obey them.

Rebuilding Jerusalem

Nehemiah lived in the palace in Persia, serving the King as his cup-bearer. When he heard that the Temple in Jerusalem had been rebuilt, but that the walls of the city were still in ruins, he was very upset. He was a Jew who cared very much for his people. He went without food for several days and prayed to God for help.

When he served wine to King Ataxerxes one evening, the King noticed that Nehemiah looked sad. "Why are you so unhappy? Are you ill?" he asked. "No, sire," replied Nehemiah. He was very frightened to speak to the king but he prayed silently to God. Then he said, "I'm sad because Jerusalem, the city of my ancestors, is in ruins. I beg you to let me go to help rebuild it."

The King agreed to let Nehemiah go; he ordered soldiers to go with him, and sent letters to the governors of the provinces Nehemiah would travel through, to see that he was safe and to give him any help he needed.

When Nehemiah reached Jerusalem, he stayed there for three days. Then, one night, he rode all around the city with a few men, looking at the walls. He didn't tell anyone what he was doing. In the morning, he went to the priests and the leaders of the people.

"Let's rebuild our city to make it great once again. We should be ashamed of the broken walls and ruined gates. God will help us," he said. He told them how his prayers had been answered, and that the King of Persia had let him come back to work in Jerusalem.

Nehemiah was appointed governor of Judah, and he organized groups of volunteers. Each family set to work on the walls and gates nearest their homes, building and repairing. Some of the people who lived there didn't want Jerusalem to be a strong city again. They jeered at the Jews and tried to stop the work.

"What do these feeble Jews think they're doing?" they asked. "Do they think they can build a city out of rubble? Even a fox could knock down these walls." The Jews worked on, encouraged by Nehemiah. "God is with us and will help us," he said.

Then the enemies of the Jews planned an attack, but Nehemiah was ready for them. Again, he prayed for God's help, and placed guards to protect the walls by day and night. During the day, half the people worked on the walls, while the other half stood guard.

The enemies tried again. They sent many messages to Nehemiah, saying, "Let's meet outside the city and talk." Nehemiah always replied, "The work is too important. I'm too busy to stop and talk."

With God's help, the work on the city walls was finished in fifty-two days. Jerusalem was a strong, walled city again. The Jews held a great celebration, marching around the city, and singing their thanks to God. Everyone was very excited and happy.

When all the people arrived at the water gate, Ezra the scholar read them the Laws of God and explained them. The people prayed to God that He would forgive them the wrongs they had done; they promised always to love Him and obey His Laws.

Brave Esther

King Xerxes was the rich and powerful ruler of the great Persian empire. When he had been king for three years, he gave a magnificent feast in his capital city of Susa. Thousands of guests were served delicious food and drank wine from gold cups. The feast lasted for seven days.

One evening, the King wanted to show his beautiful queen to his guests. "Bring Queen Vashti here to me," he ordered his servants. The Queen was holding her own feast for her women friends, and sent a message refusing to come. King Xerxes was furious. He had been made to look a fool in front of his guests, and knew that now every wife in Persia would think she could disobey her husband. He ordered Queen Vashti out of his palace, and announced that she was no longer his wife. "I'll have a new queen," he said.

King Xerxes sent his servants all over his kingdom to find the most beautiful girls so that he could choose one as his wife. A man named Mordecai worked in the King's palace. He had been brought from Judah, and had a young cousin, named Esther. He had brought her up as his own daughter after her parents had died. She was a beautiful, kind and sweet-tempered girl, so she was chosen by the King's servants.

When the King looked at all the magnificently dressed, beautiful girls, he chose Esther to be his new wife. Moradecai was delighted, but he warned Esther many times that she must never tell anyone that she was a Jewish girl, not a Persian.

One day, Mordecai overheard two men plotting to kill King Xerxes. He hurried to Esther. "You must warn your husband," he said, and told her who the two men were. Esther told the King, who had the two men put to death. He was very pleased that Esther and Mordecai had shown their loyalty to him, and ordered that Mordecai's name should be written in the palace records.

The King's chief of staff was a proud and cruel man, named Haman. He ordered that everyone had to bow down to him, but Mordecai refused. "I am a Jew, and my people and I bow down only to God," he said. Haman was very angry, and decided to get rid of Mordecai and all the Jewish people. He went to the King, and told him that some people were making trouble in his kingdom. "You may deal with them in any way you think best," said the King.

Haman ordered that Mordecai and all the other Jewish people were to be killed on a certain day. Only Mordecai knew that Queen Esther was also a Jew. He told her what Haman had ordered. "You must go to the King and beg him to save the lives of our people." Esther was very upset. "I can't go to the King," she said. "I have to wait until he sends for me. If I go to him, he may be angry and have me killed."

"God made you the Queen so that you could save us," replied Mordecai. Esther was terrified, but she bravely went to the King. Haman was there with him. She invited them both to dinner the next day. The King was pleased, and Haman felt very proud that he would dine with the King and Queen. Then he thought of Mordecai and how the Jew would not bow down to him. Angrily, he ordered that Mordecai should be hanged the next morning.

That night King Xerxes couldn't sleep. Reading through the palace records, he came across Mordecai's name and remembered that Mordecai had saved his life. "I must reward him," said the King. So, instead of being hanged in the morning, Mordecai was rewarded with rich clothes and a fine horse.

When King Xerxes and Haman went to dine with Esther that day, Esther begged the King for a kindness. The King looked at his beautiful wife. "You may have anything you wish for. You have only to ask," he said. "I and all my Jewish people are to be killed. Please save us," said Esther. The King was horrified. "Who dared to give this order?" he demanded. "It was Haman," replied Esther.

Haman flung himself down on his knees in front of Esther and begged her to save him, but King Xerxes ordered that he should be hanged. Then the King ordered that all the Jewish people were not to be killed, but were to be treated well and with respect. Esther had saved her people.

Jonah and the Whale

Jonah was a good man who usually did what God told him. One day, God told Jonah to go to the great Assyrian city of Nineveh. He was to tell the people there that God had seen they were very wicked, and that He would punish them.

Jonah didn't want to go to Nineveh. Instead, he hurried to the port of Joppa, and found that a ship was sailing to Tarshish. It was a very long way away in the opposite direction from Nineveh, and Jonah thought God wouldn't be able to see him there. He went on board the ship. As soon as it left port and sailed out onto the open sea, there was a huge storm. It had been sent by God.

The sailors were terrified, and thought they would drown. They threw everything overboard to lighten the ship which was in danger of sinking. The captain told the sailors to pray to their gods to save them.

All through the storm, Jonah lay asleep in the bottom of the ship. The captain went to him, and shook him. "Wake up, wake up and pray to your God to save us," he shouted, above the noise of the storm. Jonah sat up. "I can't pray to God because I'm running away from Him, " he shouted back.

The sailors begged Jonah to tell them how to stop the storm. "You must throw me into the sea," replied Jonah. "Then the storm will stop and the sea will grow calm again. It's because I'm running away from God that this storm has been sent." The sailors tried hard to row to the shore, but the storm got worse and worse.

At last, the
sailors decided to
throw Jonah overboard.
At once, the storm was
over, and the sailors
thanked Jonah's God for
saving their lives.

Jonah sank down and down into
the sea. Just as he thought he would
drown, a huge whale swam up and swallowed
him whole. "God sent this whale and has saved me,
but it's very dark in here," thought Jonah.

He lived inside the whale for three days. He regretted that he had
disobeyed God, and prayed that God would help him again. The
whale swam to the shore, opened its great mouth, and spat Jonah
out onto dry land. Jonah was safe.

"Now go to Nineveh," said God. Jonah set off immediately for the
city. He told the people there that unless they gave up their wicked
ways, God would destroy the city in forty days' time.

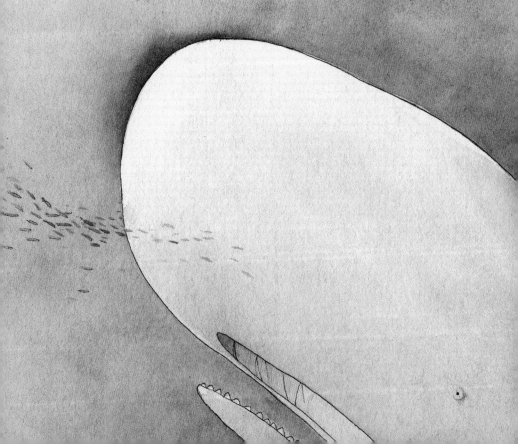

The people listened to Jonah, and the King ordered them to be
sorry for the way they had behaved, and to pray to God.

Jonah sat outside the city and waited for it to be destroyed. He
was very hot and angry. He wanted God to destroy Nineveh. But
God saw that the people had turned to Him, and He saved the city.
"Jonah," said God, "I love all people and I am everywhere. You
can't run away from Me." And Jonah knew that this was true.

The Old Testament Ends

The Jews rebuilt the Temple and the walls and houses of
Jerusalem under the leadership of Ezra and Nehemiah. But the
new Temple was not nearly as magnificent as the one King
Solomon had built, and the Jews had to share the land with
other peoples. The glorious days of Israel under King David
and King Solomon were never seen again.

The Jews still did not obey God fully, despite all that He had
done for them: rescuing them from Egypt, giving them the laws
when Moses was leader, and helping them conquer the
Promised Land under Joshua. Even after Ezra had read all the
laws to the Jews, Nehemiah still found people, including the
priests, breaking God's commandments.

Four hundred years passed after the Jews returned to
Jerusalem, and during this time many changes took place in
the Middle East. The Greeks took control from the Persians,
and later the Romans took over from them. God had told the
Jews he would send a special man to save them.

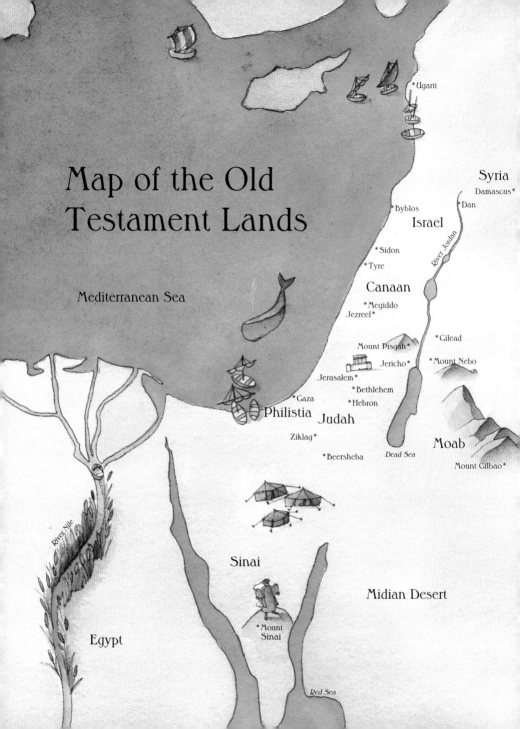

Map of the Old
Testament Lands

*Ugarit

Syria

Damascus*

*Byblos   *Dan

Israel

Mediterranean Sea

*Sidon

*Tyre

Canaan

River Jordan

*Megiddo

Jezreel*

*Gilead

Mount Pisgah*

*Mount Nebo

Jericho*

Jerusalem*

*Bethlehem

*Gaza

*Hebron

Philistia   Judah

Ziklag*

Moab

*Beersheba

Dead Sea

Mount Gilbao*

Sinai

Midian Desert

River Nile

*Mount
Sinai

Egypt

Red Sea

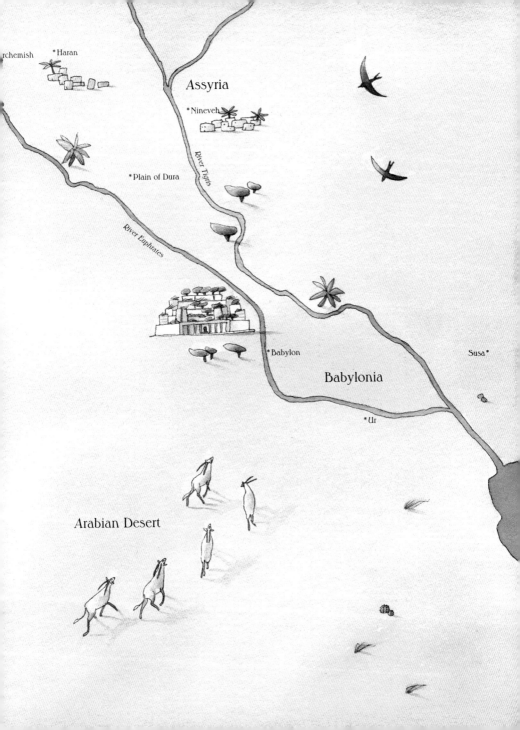

THE
NEW
TESTAMENT

Mary and the Angel

In the little town of Nazareth among the hills of Galilee, in northern
Israel, lived a young woman. Her name was Mary and she was
soon to be married to Joseph, a carpenter who lived in the same
town. One day, when Mary was alone, she was very surprised to see
an angel suddenly appear in front of her.

"Don't be frightened, Mary," said the angel. "I am Gabriel
and I've been sent by God to give you a message.
You will have a son, and you must call him
Jesus. He will be a great King and his
kingdom will last forever."

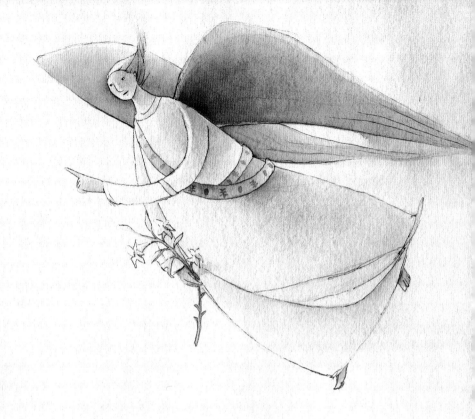

"I don't understand," said Mary, very puzzled. "How can I have a son when I'm not even married yet?"

"It will be the work of God," replied Gabriel. "Everyone thought your cousin Elizabeth could never have children, but she is expecting a baby soon. God can do anything. Your son will be holy and will be the Son of God."

Mary still didn't understand, but she trusted God. She bowed her head and said, "I'm God's servant and I'll do what He wants." Then she looked up, but Gabriel had gone.

Elizabeth and Zechariah

A few days later, Mary set off on the long journey to visit her cousin, Elizabeth, who lived with her husband, Zechariah. As soon as she arrived, Mary began to tell Elizabeth all that had happened to her. To Mary's surprise, she found Elizabeth already knew Mary was to have a baby.

"It's wonderful that God has chosen you to be the mother of his Son," Elizabeth said, and then she told Mary her own news. She and Zechariah had, for many years, prayed to God, asking him for a child, but she had had no baby. Zechariah was a priest and, one day when he was taking part in a service, he was chosen to burn incense at the altar in the Temple. While he was alone, an angel appeared by the altar. He was very frightened.

"Don't be afraid, Zechariah," said the angel. "God has heard your prayers, and has sent me to tell you that you and Elizabeth will have a son. You are to call him John. He will make you very happy. God has chosen him to tell the people that their King is coming, and to help them to be ready for him."

"This can't be true. My wife and I are much too old now to have children," said Zechariah.

"I am Gabriel, who has been sent by God to tell you this good news. Because you don't believe it, you'll be struck dumb. You won't speak again until God's promise comes true."

When he had finished his duties in the Temple, Zechariah went home to Elizabeth, but he couldn't speak. He wrote down all that had happened and to explain why he was dumb. She was very worried about him, and stayed quietly in her house.

"God has kept his promise," Elizabeth said to Mary. "My baby is due in four months' time." Mary stayed with Elizabeth and Zechariah for three months, and then went home to Nazareth.

Elizabeth had her baby, a son. Everyone wanted to call him Zechariah after his father, but Elizabeth said his name was John. "No one in our family has the name John," said her family.

Zechariah picked up his writing tablet, and wrote, "His name is John." At that moment, Zechariah could speak again, and he could thank God out aloud for his little son.

The Birth of Jesus

Mary returned to Nazareth and to Joseph, to whom she was engaged. Joseph had heard she was going to have a baby. He was very worried. He was a kind man, but he felt it wasn't right that he should marry her.

One night, he had a dream. In it, an angel told him that Mary had done nothing wrong, and that he should marry her. Her son was the Son of God. He was to be called Jesus, and he would save the people from God's punishment for the wrong things they had done.

The next morning, Joseph remembered what the angel had said to him in his dream. He made arrangements for the wedding, and soon he and Mary were married. Joseph vowed that he would always take care of Mary and her son.

Mary and Joseph lived happily together in Nazareth, looking forward to the birth of Mary's baby. A few months later, the Roman Emperor Augustus, who ruled Israel, made a new law. Everyone must go to the town their family came from, to register so they could be taxed. Joseph's family was descended from King David, and so he had to travel to Bethlehem, where David was born.

Joseph packed up food, water and warm clothes, and clothes for the baby, and loaded them onto his donkey. Then he and Mary began the long journey, which took many days, across the hills of Galilee to Bethlehem. It was late evening when they arrived, and Mary was very tired. She knew her baby would be born soon.

The streets were noisy and crowded with people who had come to register. Joseph tried to find a room for them to stay in for the night, but every inn they stopped at was already full. He trudged through the cold, dark streets, leading the donkey which carried Mary.

When they came to the last inn, the inn-keeper told them that all his rooms were already taken, but there was a stable nearby they could shelter in for the night.

Joseph led the donkey to the stable. He gently helped Mary down, and unloaded their things. Then he spread out clean straw on the floor to make a soft bed for her, and covered it with his cloak. Mary ate a little food and lay down, thankful that she could rest at last.

That night Mary's baby was born. She washed him and wrapped him in the clothes she had brought with her. Joseph filled a manger with soft, clean hay to make a bed for the baby, and Mary laid him in it. She called her new son Jesus, as the angel had told her, and she knew he was the Son of God.

On the hills outside Bethlehem, a group of shepherds lay around their camp fire, guarding their sheep from wild animals during the night. Suddenly, they saw a dazzling glow lighting up the dark sky. As they watched, it grew brighter and brighter, and an angel appeared in front of them; they felt very scared.

"Don't be frightened," said the angel. "I have wonderful news for you, and for all people. Tonight the Son of God was born. You will find him lying in a manger in Bethlehem." As the shepherds stared in amazement, a great crowd of angels appeared, singing praises to God. "Glory to God in the highest, and peace on earth to all people who love Him," they sang. Then the light faded, the angels were gone, and the night was dark again.

When they had recovered from their astonishment, the shepherds wondered what they should do. "We must go to Bethlehem and look for this child we've been told about," said one. The others agreed. Very excited, they quickly packed up their things and, leaving their sheep, they hurried down the dark hills to the little town.

They soon found the stable and, knocking on the door, crept quietly in. They looked at the baby, and knelt down in front of the manger. Then they told Mary and Joseph what the angel had said to them.

After a while, they got to their feet and left the stable. Once outside, they strode through the streets of Bethlehem, telling everyone they met the good news that the Son of God had been born that night. By the morning, the whole town knew about the birth of Jesus. Singing praises to God and full of wonder, the shepherds walked back to their sheep.

In the dimly-lit stable, Mary gazed at her baby. She thought about what the shepherds had told her the angel had said, and wondered what it all meant.

Following a Star

In a country far away to the east of Bethlehem, there were wise men who studied the stars. One night they saw a new star that was much brighter than all the others. They knew that this meant something special had happened. After consulting all their books, they decided that it was a sign that a new ruler had been born, and that they must go to find him.

They prepared for a long journey, and set off, carrying presents for this new ruler. Every night they followed the star which moved across the sky ahead of them.

At last, they arrived in the great city of Jerusalem. There they asked, "Where can we find the baby who is born to be King of the Jews? We have seen his star and have come to worship him."

When King Herod heard that these strangers were looking for the baby King, he was very worried. The Roman rulers of Israel had made him King of the Jews, and he was frightened that a new king would try to take his throne. He sent for the priests and learned men, and asked them where this baby was born.

After much study of all the old writings and records, they told King Herod that, many years ago, it had been foretold that one day the King of the Jews would be born in Bethlehem.

King Herod called the wise men to a secret meeting with him. When they came, he told them to go to Bethlehem. "When you find this child, come back and tell me, so that I may worship him too," he said. The wise men agreed, and started to travel along the road to Bethlehem. The star still moved ahead of them and then seemed to stop over the town. The wise men knew then that they had come to the right place.

They soon found where Mary and Joseph were living. When the wise men saw the baby, they knelt down in front of him, and gave Mary the presents they had brought with them. The presents were gold, sweet-smelling frankincense, and a special ointment called myrrh. Then they quietly got to their feet and left the stable.

On their way back to Jerusalem and King Herod, they camped outside Bethlehem. That night, they had a dream in which an angel warned them not to return to King Herod. In the morning, they loaded up their camels and took a different road back to their own country, avoiding Jerusalem.

One night, Joseph also had a dream. In it, an angel warned him that Jesus was in great danger, and that he must take Mary and the baby to Egypt where they would be safe. "Go at once," said the angel. "Stay in Egypt until I tell you that the danger has passed." Joseph woke Mary, and quickly packed up their things, loading them onto their donkey. Carrying Jesus, they began their long journey through the desert while it was still dark.

King Herod waited for the wise men to come back to Jerusalem. When he realized he'd been tricked, he was furious. He ordered his soldiers to march to Bethlehem and kill all the boys under two years old. In that way, he was sure that Jesus, the King of the Jews, would die. The soldiers carried out the dreadful task. The people had always hated this cruel King appointed by their Roman rulers, but now they hated him even more.

Mary, Joseph and Jesus lived safely in Egypt. After a while, Joseph had another dream in which an angel told him that King Herod had died, and it was safe for him to take Mary and Jesus home. After another very long journey, they reached Nazareth, and settled down in their own house again.

Jesus in the Temple

Every year, Mary and Joseph went to Jerusalem to celebrate the Feast of the Passover with many other Jews. It reminded them of the time, all those years ago, when Moses, with the help of God, had freed the Hebrew people from slavery in Egypt and led them to the land God had promised them.

When Jesus was twelve, he went with them to Jerusalem to celebrate the Passover as usual. After the festival was over, Mary and Joseph joined their friends for the journey back to Nazareth. They thought Jesus was walking with the other boys and it wasn't until the evening that they realized he was missing. They asked everyone if they knew where Jesus was, but no one had seen him.

Early the next morning, Mary and Joseph hurried back to Jerusalem, desperate with worry. For three days, they anxiously searched the city streets for Jesus, but couldn't find him. At last, they saw him sitting in the Temple with the Temple teachers, listening to them, and asking them questions. The teachers were amazed that Jesus, who was only twelve, understood so much of what they told him, and were astonished by the questions he asked. Mary and Joseph were very surprised to find him there.

"Why did you do this to us?" Mary asked Jesus. "We've been so worried about you. We've searched everywhere. We thought we'd never find you." Jesus looked at his mother. "I didn't mean to cause you so much trouble," he said. "Didn't you know I would be here, in my Father's house?"

He went back to Nazereth with them, but Mary kept remembering all that happened in Jerusalem. Jesus grew up to be a wise and strong young man who loved and obeyed his parents and God.

Jesus is Baptized

Jesus lived in Nazareth with Mary and Joseph
until he was about thirty years old. Then he went to
the Jordan River where his cousin John, the son of
Elizabeth and Zechariah, was teaching the people about God.
Crowds of people came to listen when John told them that they
should do as God wanted, and that they should be ready for His
King who was coming soon.

When they asked what they should do, John told them to share
their food with the hungry, to give their spare clothes to those who
needed them, and that the tax collectors should demand no more
from the people than was due.

John led the people who wanted to live better lives down to the
river. There he baptized them with water, as a sign that the bad
things they had done were washed away, and they could make a
new, clean start. "I baptize you with water," John said to them, "but
one is coming who is much greater than I. I'm not worthy to undo
his sandals. He will baptize you with the Holy Spirit."

Jesus went to John and asked John to baptize him, but John
said, "It's not right that I should baptize you. You should baptize
me." Jesus said to John, "Let us do what God wants." After saying
a prayer, Jesus walked into the river. John poured water over him
to show that he had been washed clean. Then, just as Jesus
stepped out of the Jordan, the Holy Spirit came in the form of a
white dove and hovered over him, and he heard the voice of God
say to him, "You are my dear Son. I am very pleased with you."

Jesus and his Disciples

Jesus went to Capernaum, a town near Lake Galilee. There he talked to the people about God, and healed the ones who were ill. News of his teaching spread quickly and, everywhere he went, people crowded around him to hear what he had to tell them.

One day, Jesus was walking along the shore of the lake. As usual, crowds of people came to listen to him. There was a boat pulled up on the shore owned by two fishermen, Peter and his brother, Andrew. Jesus climbed on board. "Please push the boat onto the water and row a little way out on the lake so I can speak to the people," he said. The two men did as he asked.

After Jesus had spoken to the people, he told Peter and Andrew to row farther away from the shore and put out their fishing nets. "It's no good. We fished all night and caught nothing," said Peter, "but we'll do as you say." When he and Andrew began to pull in the nets, they were so full of fish, the nets were almost breaking.

Peter and Andrew shouted across to two other fishermen, James and John, in their boat. "Come and help us," they called. James and John helped them to pull in the nets. Together they filled both boats with fish.

When the four men saw how many fish they'd caught, they were very frightened and knelt down in front of Jesus. "Don't be afraid," said Jesus. "Come with me, and I will make you fishermen of people."

Peter and Andrew, James and John rowed their two boats back to shore and unloaded the fish. Then they left their boats and went with Jesus on his journeys through the towns and villages around Lake Galilee.

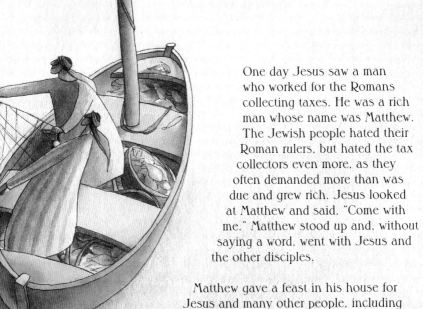

One day Jesus saw a man who worked for the Romans collecting taxes. He was a rich man whose name was Matthew. The Jewish people hated their Roman rulers, but hated the tax collectors even more, as they often demanded more than was due and grew rich. Jesus looked at Matthew and said, "Come with me." Matthew stood up and, without saying a word, went with Jesus and the other disciples.

Matthew gave a feast in his house for Jesus and many other people, including tax collectors. Some of the religious Jewish people saw Jesus there. They asked his friends why such a good man as Jesus would sit down and eat with so many bad people. Jesus heard the question, and answered, "Healthy people don't need a doctor. It's the sick who need help. I've come to ask the bad people to change their ways. The good people don't need me."

One evening, Jesus walked high up a mountain and stayed all night, praying to God. In the morning, he came down again and he chose twelve disciples to help with his work. As well as Peter, Andrew, James, John and Matthew, there was Philip and Bartholomew, Thomas, another James, Simon, Judas and Judas Iscariot. These twelve men became his special friends and followers. They went everywhere with him, listening to his teachings and watching the wonderful things he did. He told them what God had sent him to do.

A Wedding in Cana

When Jesus was in Galilee, he and some friends were invited to a wedding in the town of Cana. Mary, his mother, was there. Long before the wedding feast was over, the wine was finished and there wasn't any more. Mary went to Jesus and told him what had happened. Then she said to the servants, "Do whatever he tells you to do."

There were six huge water jugs near the entrance so that the people could wash before eating the meal, as the Jewish law instructed. Now the jugs were empty.

Jesus said to the servants, "Fill up the jugs with water," and soon the servants had filled them to the top. Then he said, "Pour out some of the water and take it to the man who is organizing the feast." The servants did as Jesus told them. The ruler of the feast tasted the water and found that it was wine. He didn't know that it had come from a water jug, but the servants knew.

The ruler turned to the bridegroom. "Everyone serves good wine at the beginning of a feast and, when everybody has drunk well, he serves the ordinary wine," he said. "But you've kept the best wine until now."

This was the first of the many wonderful things that Jesus did, and it strengthened the belief of his disciples who saw it and they listened to what Jesus told them.

Sermon on the Mountain

Everywhere Jesus went with his disciples, people gathered around
him to hear his teachings. On the Sabbath he spoke to them in
the synagogues, but on other days he spoke to them outdoors as
the weather was mostly hot and dry.

One day, he walked a little way up a mountain. The people sat
down on the ground so they could see and hear him. Jesus
told them that those people who were really hungry to know
God would be satisfied. He said they should be content
with what they had, and not to worry about food,
clothing or money.

"You think that rich people are happy
because they have everything they want,
but you are wrong. Only those who love
God will have everything. Those of you
who are poor will have riches in Heaven.
Those of you who are sad will be happy in
God's kingdom. For those of you who have been
hated and despised because you are my friends,
there is a great reward waiting for you in Heaven.

"Don't try to save up lots of money; someone will only steal it.
Other things you might hoard will only rust and rot away. Store up
your treasure with God, where no one can rob you of it. You can't
spend your life trying to become rich, and do want God wants.
You can only do one or the other.

"Look at the birds," he said. "They don't grow and store food, but God takes care of them and He will take care of you. Look at the beautiful flowers. They don't make their clothes but not even the great King Solomon was better or more brightly dressed than they are. Don't worry about the future and what might or might not happen. Do what God wants you to do. Trust Him, and He will give you what you need.

"You have the laws of God and I haven't come to change them. The law says that you mustn't kill anyone, but if you think murderous thoughts about someone, that is as bad as killing. You may want revenge for a wrong someone has done you, to pay back what you have received. But God wants you to love your enemies, to repay a wrong with kindness. It is not easy to follow God's path but you must start on the journey.

"Don't hide your good qualities, but let them shine out in your lives. You are like lamps. No one lights a lamp and puts it under a bowl. They place it where it lights up a dark house. When people see the good things you do, they will thank God.

"It's easy to love your family and your friends, but you should love all people, even those who hate you and want to harm you. When you do someone a good turn, don't tell everybody about it. Keep it a secret. God will see you and He will reward you.

"When you pray to God, don't make a great, noisy display of it. Do it quietly when you are alone. Talk to God as you would to a father who loves you. Don't make your prayers long to show off or use meaningless words. God hears you and knows what you need.

"When you talk to God, say this prayer to Him:

>   Our Father who is in Heaven
>   Holy is Your name,
>   May Your Kingdom come,
>   May Your will be done on earth as it is in Heaven.
>   Give us our food each day,
>   Forgive us the wrong things we have done
>   As we forgive the wrongs others have done to us,
>   Do not let us be tempted to do wrong,
>   But save us from evil.

"Anyone who listens to me," said Jesus, "and does what I say, is like a man who builds a house on a rock. When it rains, the wind blows and the floods come, his house will stand strong and firm. But anyone who listens to me and doesn't do what I say is like a man who builds his house on the sand. When it rains, the wind blows, and the floods come, his house will be washed away because it was built, not on solid rock, but on soft sand."

The Disabled Man

News that Jesus was teaching people about God and making the ill ones well again spread very quickly. Wherever he went with his twelve disciples, people journeyed from all over the country and from the great city of Jerusalem to listen to him and to be healed of all kinds of diseases.

One day, when Jesus was again in Capernaum, he sat in a house that was so packed with people, no one could get in or out of the door. Four friends carried a man, who couldn't move, to the house on a stretcher. When they found they couldn't get in through the door, they carried the stretcher up onto the flat roof of the house. There they made a hole in the roof and used ropes to lower the man on his stretcher down into the room where Jesus was sitting.

Jesus looked up at the four friends peering through the hole in the roof and saw the faith they had in him. Then he looked at the man on the stretcher. "My son," he said, "your sins are forgiven."

The Jewish leaders who heard Jesus say this whispered angrily to each other. Jesus had no right to forgive sins, they said; only God could do that. Jesus heard what they were saying. He looked at them and asked them, "Is it easier to forgive a man for the wrong things he has done, or to make him walk again? To show you that I have the power to forgive sins . . ."

Jesus stopped and turned to the man on
the stretcher. "Get up, pick up your stretcher
and go home," he said.

Without saying a word, the man at once stood up and, taking his
stretcher with him, he pushed his way out of the house. Watched
by his four delighted friends on the roof, he walked home,
saying a prayer of thanks to God.

The people in the house stared at Jesus, amazed and a
little frightened. They had never seen anything like
this before. Very excited, they whispered to each
other and said prayers of praise to God.

The Centurion's Servant

Jesus and his disciples journeyed through the country talking to the people. When they returned to the city of Capernaum, some of the Jewish leaders came to meet them. They had been sent to Jesus by a Roman soldier, a centurion, to ask him to come to heal the soldier's much-loved servant who was very ill. "This centurion is a good man," they said. "He has been very good to our people, and has built a synagogue for them."

Jesus went with them to the centurion's house, but before he reached it the Roman came out to meet him. "Lord," he said, "don't bother to come any further. I know I'm not good enough to stand in front of you or to invite you into my house. I'm a man of authority, used to giving orders to the men I command and to having them obeyed. I know that you only have to say the word and my servant will be well again."

Jesus was amazed by what the soldier said to him. He turned to the people who had followed him, and said, "Look at this man. I haven't found anyone in Israel with a stronger faith." Then he said to the centurion, "Go back to your servant. Because of your faith, he has been healed." When the soldier and the Jewish leaders went into the house, they found that the servant was completely well again.

A Storm on the Lake

One evening Jesus asked some of his disciples to take him in a boat across Lake Galilee. He had been talking to the people all day and healing the ill ones, and he was very tired. When the disciples pushed the boat out onto the water, Jesus lay down and was soon fast asleep.

The lake was very calm, with just a gentle breeze blowing. The disciples hoisted the sail and the boat skimmed away across the smooth water. When it was far from the shore, the wind started blowing stronger and stronger, until there was a great storm. The waves grew higher and higher, splashing into the boat.

The disciples were very scared. Some of them had been fishermen and knew how dangerous storms on the lake could be. They were afraid the boat would fill with water and sink. Although the noise of the wind was very loud and the boat was tossed around by the waves, Jesus didn't stir.

At last, one of the disciples could bear it no longer. He shook Jesus to wake him up. "Master, please save us," he shouted "Can't you see that we're all going to drown?"

Jesus woke up and looked at
the storm for a moment. Then he
stood up, raised his arm and said,
"Hush, be still." At once the wind
dropped, the waves subsided, and the
lake was calm again. "Why were you
afraid?" Jesus asked his disciples. "Don't
you believe that I will take care of you?"
The disciples didn't know what to say.
They felt a little afraid of Jesus. They
whispered to each other, "Who is this
man that even the wind and the waves
obey his commands?" The boat
sailed gently on, and Jesus and
his disciples safely reached the
far shore of the lake.

The Death of John

While Jesus was teaching in the towns and villages around Lake Galilee, his cousin John, who had become known as John the Baptist, was talking to the people about God and baptizing them. He also spoke against King Herod Antipas because the King had married his brother's wife, Herodias. This, said John, was wrong.

King Herod had John arrested and thrown into prison. Queen Herodias wanted the King to kill John, but Herod knew John was a good and holy man, and was afraid to have him executed.

When King Herod had a birthday, he gave a feast for his lords, captains and other important people. Salome, the young and beautiful daughter of Queen Herodias, danced to entertain the guests. The King was so delighted with her performance, he promised, "Ask me for anything you wish. You may even have half my kingdom."

Queen Herodias saw her chance. She whispered to her daughter, "Ask him for the head of John the Baptist to be brought to you on a dish." The girl repeated this to the King.

Herod was dismayed. He didn't want to kill John, but he had made his promise in front of all his guests and he couldn't break it. He ordered his guards to go to the prison, and to cut off John's head. It was then brought in on a dish and presented to Salome who gave it to her mother. When John's friends heard what had happened, they took away his body and buried it. Then they went to tell the news to Jesus, who was very sad at the death of his cousin.

The Good Shepherd

When Jesus was talking to the people, he often told them stories so that they could understand more easily what he was trying to teach them. He said to the men, women and children who came to listen to him, "If you have ears, hear what I say."

One day, Jesus told them a new story. "If a shepherd has a hundred sheep to look after and one of them wanders off and gets lost, what does the shepherd do?" he asked. "He leaves his ninety-nine sheep," Jesus went on, "where he knows they'll be safe from hungry wild animals, and goes to look for the one missing sheep.

"The shepherd searches everywhere for that one sheep, listening all the time to hear it bleating. However long it takes, he doesn't give up until he finds it. Then he picks up the sheep, puts it on his shoulders and carries it home, delighted that he can take it safely back to the rest of the flock. Then he calls his family and his friends to come and celebrate with him that he has found his one lost sheep.

"There is more joy in Heaven," continued Jesus, "when someone who has disobeyed God and led a bad life is sorry for what he or she has done, and comes back to live as God wants them to do.

"I am like that good shepherd," Jesus told the people. "I look after my people as if they were my sheep. I never run away and leave them when wolves try to kill and eat them. The sheep know my voice and follow me. I lead them and protect them. I am ready to die for them."

The Daughter of Jairus

When Jesus was walking with his disciples through a town one day, Jairus, a ruler of the synagogue ran up to him and knelt down in front of him. "My little daughter is very ill. I think she's dying. Please will you come to my house and put your hands on her so that she may get better?" he asked.

As Jesus began to follow Jairus, a woman pushed through the crowd around Jesus to get near him. She had been ill for twelve years and none of the doctors had been able to cure her. She had heard of Jesus. "If only I could just touch his clothes, I know I would get better at last," she thought. When she was close enough, she put out her hand and touched him. At once, she was completely cured. Jesus looked at the people around him. "Who touched me?" he asked, knowing that someone had been healed.

The woman was very frightened. Trembling, she knelt down in front of Jesus and told him that when she touched him she had been cured of her illness. Jesus looked down at the woman. "Your faith has made you well," he said, smiling. "Go in peace."

Jesus went with Jairus to his house, followed by a crowd of people. Before he reached the house, someone came running out. Weeping, she cried to Jairus, "You are too late. Your little daughter is dead. Don't ask Jesus to come."

"She is not dead. She is asleep," said Jesus, and he walked on to the house with three disciples, Peter, James and John. Jesus asked everyone else to leave the house, except the girl's mother and father. Then he went into her room, gently took her hand, and said "Little girl, get up."

At once, the girl opened her eyes and got up off her bed. The girl's parents were astonished and overjoyed to see their daughter alive and well again. "Now give her something to eat," said Jesus, "but tell no one about this." Then he and his three disciples quietly left the house.

The Sower

One day, when Jesus was talking to the people on the shore of Lake Galilee, so many crowded around to hear him, he pushed a boat out on the water and sat down in it. The people settled down on the shore to listen. Jesus told them this story.

"There was a farmer who went out to sow his field with corn. As he walked along, he scattered seeds over the ground, but some of them fell on the stony path and were soon eaten up by the birds. This is like people who hear the word of God, but don't take in its message. Satan will soon make them forget what they have heard.

"Some of the seeds fell where the soil was thin and stony. The corn grew too quickly because it didn't have good roots; it was scorched by the sun, dried up and died. This is like the people who gladly accept the word of God, but don't think about it. When they get into trouble or difficulties, they soon give up their faith.

"Some of the seeds dropped among thistles and weeds which grew up around them and choked them. This is like the people who are choked by their worries, love of money or love of pleasure and forget God's word.

"Some of the seeds fell on good, rich soil. The corn grew high and ripened into a fine harvest. This is like the people who listen to and understand God's message. The way they live their lives shows that they love God and obey Him. They do much good and will be well rewarded."

The Cruel Servant

Peter, one of the disciples, asked Jesus, "Lord, how many times should I forgive someone who has wronged me? Should it be up to seven times?"

"Not seven times, but seventy times seven," answered Jesus, and to explain what he meant, he told this story to his disciples.

"There was a king who was very kind to his servants, and would lend them money when they needed it. When he found that one servant owed him a huge sum of money, he had the man brought to him. As the man couldn't repay the money, the king ordered that all the servant's possessions should be seized and that he, his wife, and his children should be sold as slaves.

"The servant fell on his knees in front of the King and begged, 'Lord, please be patient with me and I'll repay everything I owe you.' The King felt sorry for the man; he allowed the servant to go free without repaying the debt.

"When that servant found that another
servant couldn't repay him a very
small sum of money he had borrowed
from him, he grabbed the man by the
throat and demanded, 'Pay me what you
owe me now.' The servant fell on his
knees and begged for time to pay.

"The first servant had no mercy; he had the
man thrown into prison until he could pay the debt.
The other servants were very upset by the way the cruel servant
behaved, and went to tell the King.

"The King sent for the cruel servant. 'You are a wicked man,' he
said angrily. 'When you begged for mercy and time to pay, I
forgave you your huge debt, but when my other servant couldn't
pay you a tiny debt, you showed him no mercy. You should have
forgiven him in the same way that I forgave you.' The King ordered
that the cruel servant should be put in prison until he could repay
all his huge debt.

"That is how my heavenly Father will treat each of you unless
you forgive, from the bottom of your heart, anyone who has
treated you badly."

Feeding the Hungry Crowd

One day Jesus was feeling tired. He had been talking to the people all day and healing them, and he wanted to go to a quiet place to have a little time to himself. He and his disciples boarded a boat and sailed across Lake Galilee to a lonely beach. There they landed, pulled the boat up onto the shore and walked up a hill to rest.

Although they were alone, some people had seen where they went, and the news that Jesus was there quickly spread. Soon people started to walk from the towns and villages to see him, and to be cured of their diseases.

The disciples wanted to send the people away, but Jesus felt sorry for the people. He walked among them, talking to them, answering their questions and making the ill ones well again. More and more arrived until there were thousands of them.

In the evening, a disciple said to Jesus, "It's time these people went home. Send them away now so they can find food. There is nothing here for them to eat."

"They are hungry. We must feed them first," said Jesus. "There is nowhere to buy food, and even a huge amount of money would not buy enough bread for all these people," said Philip, one of the disciples.

Andrew, another of the disciples, said to Jesus, "There is a boy here who has five small barley loaves and two fish, but that's not much for all these people." Jesus looked down at the boy. "May I take your food?" he asked. "Yes, Master," said the boy, and gladly gave it to Jesus.

"Tell the people to sit down on the grass in groups," Jesus said to the disciples. The disciples walked through the crowd asking them all to sit down. Altogether, there were about five thousand men, women and children.

Jesus held up the boy's five small loaves and two small fish, and said a prayer of thanks to God. Then he broke up the bread and fish into pieces and handed them to the disciples. "Give them to the people," he said.

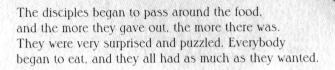

The disciples began to pass around the food,
and the more they gave out, the more there was.
They were very surprised and puzzled. Everybody
began to eat, and they all had as much as they wanted.

When the meal was over, Jesus said to the disciples, "Collect
up all the leftover food. Nothing must be wasted." The disciples
walked over the hillside, picking up the pieces of bread and fish.
When they'd finished, they'd filled twelve baskets with food.

The Good Samaritan

When Jesus was teaching the people about God, a clever lawyer stood up and asked him a question, trying to trap him. "What should I do to gain eternal life?" asked the lawyer. "What does the law say you should do?" Jesus asked him. "You must love God with all your heart, with all your soul, with all your strength and with all your mind," replied the lawyer. "And you must love other people as much as you love yourself. But who are these people?"

Jesus answered the lawyer by telling him this story. "A Jew who lived in Jerusalem left the city and began the long walk to Jericho. Although the Jew knew it was dangerous to travel alone, because there were robbers on the road, he went on his own.

"When the Jew came to a lonely stretch of the road, some thieves were waiting for someone to rob. They rushed out of their hiding place and attacked him. They beat him, knocked him down and kicked him. Then they stole all he had with him and ran away, leaving him lying on the ground, badly wounded.

"After a while, a priest who served in the Temple in Jerusalem came down the road. He saw the Jew lying in the dust, but he dug his heels into his donkey's sides and trotted quickly away.

"A little later, a man who worked in the Temple came by. He looked at the wounded man as he passed, but he didn't stop. He hurried away down the road.

"Then a Samaritan trotted past on his donkey. Everyone knows the Samaritans and the Jews have always hated each other, but this Samaritan felt sorry for the Jew. He stopped immediately and got off his donkey. Then he opened his pack and, kneeling in the dust beside the man, he poured oil on the Jew's wounds to ease the pain, and wine to heal them. Then he bandaged up the wounds with strips of cloth.

"When he had done everything he could, the Samaritan lifted the Jew up on his donkey and led it down the road to an inn. There he put the Jew to bed and bought him some supper.

"The next morning, the Samaritan paid the innkeeper and said, 'Look after this man for me and I'll pay you any extra money I owe you when I come this way again.'

"Now," Jesus asked the lawyer, "which of these three men do you think was kind to the man who was attacked by robbers?"

"The Samaritan, of course," answered the lawyer. "Go and be like that Samaritan. Be kind to everyone," said Jesus, "not just your family and your friends, but everyone."

Mary, Martha and Lazarus

When Jesus arrived in the village of Bethany, near the city of Jerusalem, he stayed with two sisters, Mary and Martha, and their brother, Lazarus. Lazarus was out of the house, but Mary sat quietly at Jesus' feet listening to him, while Martha hurried about getting the house ready and preparing a meal.

After a while, Martha grew resentful that she did all the work and Mary did nothing. "Don't you care, Lord, that Mary leaves everything to me?" she complained to Jesus. "Tell her to come and help me."

"Martha," said Jesus gently, "you worry too much about taking care of the house. Mary is wise. It's more important that she listens to my teaching than is busy with cooking and housework."

A little while after Jesus had left the house in Bethany, Lazarus became seriously ill. Mary and Martha sent a message to Jesus telling him about Lazarus and asking him to come to save their brother's life. They expected Jesus to arrive at once, but they waited for two days and still Jesus didn't come.

When Jesus received the message, he was with his disciples. "Our friend Lazarus is asleep. I'll go and wake him up," he said. "If he's asleep, won't he get better?" asked one of the disciples. Jesus knew that Lazarus was now dead. Jesus waited several days and then returned to Bethany.

When he and his disciples reached the house at last. Lazarus had been in his tomb for four days. Mary stayed in the house weeping with her friends, but Martha ran out to meet Jesus. "Lord, if you'd been here, my brother wouldn't have died," she cried.

"He will live again," said Jesus. "I know he will when God brings all the dead back to life on the last day," sobbed Martha. "Everyone who trusts in me will live forever, even if they die. Don't you believe that?" Jesus asked her. "Yes, Lord, I believe you are the Son of God who has come into the world," replied Martha.

Then Martha went into the house and said quietly to Mary, "The Master has come and is asking for you." Still crying, Mary walked out of the house, with the friends who had come to comfort her. When Jesus saw how heartbroken she was, he felt deeply sorry for her, and also wept. "Take me to Lazarus," he said gently.

They led him to the tomb which was in a cave. In front of it was a big rock sealing up the tomb. "Move away the rock," said Jesus. "But Lazarus has been dead for four days. He'll smell bad," said Martha. "I told you that if you trust me, you will see God's glory," Jesus answered her.

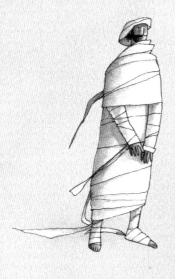

Friends of the two sisters rolled away the rock from in front of the tomb. Jesus walked up to it. He said a prayer to God and then shouted, "Lazarus, come out."

To everyone's astonishment, Lazarus walked out of the tomb, alive and well, still wrapped in his grave clothes which covered his body and face. "Unwrap him and let him go," said Jesus. Lazarus was just like a man who had only been asleep, not one who had died and come back to life.

The people who saw this believed Jesus had been sent to them by God. Some went to the Jewish leaders, the Pharisees, and told them what had happened. The Pharisees had a meeting with the Chief Priest. "We must put a stop to this," they decided, "or everyone will believe in Jesus. Then the Romans will suspect the Jewish people will rebel against them and destroy our nation. It's better that one man should die, than a whole nation."

From that day on, they often met together to plan how they could kill Jesus.

Vision on a Mountain

Many people had listened to Jesus teaching them about God, and seen the wonderful things he had done. Jesus asked his twelve disciples, "Who do the people say I am?"

"Some say you are John the Baptist come alive again, and some say you are a prophet, perhaps Elijah," replied the disciples. "And who do you say I am?" asked Jesus. Peter answered at once, "You are the promised King, the Son of God."

Jesus was very pleased with Peter's answer. "Peter, you are blessed, for God Himself has given you this understanding. You are the rock on which I will build my Church," he said. Now Jesus could prepare his disciples for what was to come.

"Soon I shall have to go to Jerusalem. There they won't accept me as God's King. They will try me, condemn me and put me to death but, after three days, I will live again."

Then he warned his disciples that they too would have to suffer. "Anyone who follows me," he said, "must give up the riches and comfort of this world, but they will be greatly rewarded in Heaven."

About a week later, Jesus took Peter, James and John with him up high on a mountain to pray. Suddenly the three disciples saw Jesus change; his face shone like the sun and his clothes looked as white as snow. Then two other shining figures appeared and talked to Jesus. They were Moses and the prophet Elijah.

The disciples were terrified. Then a bright cloud drifted over the sky, and a voice said, "This is my Son. Listen to him." The cloud passed, and the disciples were alone again on the mountain with Jesus. As they walked down the mountain, Jesus said, "Tell no one what you have seen today until my Father brings me back to life again after my death."

The Prodigal Son

Jesus was talking to some people when a group of Pharisees joined the crowd. They muttered to each other, "Why does this man keep on talking and eating with people he knows have bad ways?" Jesus heard them and reminded them, "When only one person is sorry for the wrong things he has done and wants to obey God, there is joy in Heaven." Then he told them this story.

"A rich farmer had two sons. One day, the younger son said, 'Father, half of everything you have will be mine one day. I want you to give it to me now.' The father was very upset by his son's demand, but he did as he was asked; he counted out and gave his son a great deal of his money.

"A few days later, the son rode away to a distant city, taking the money with him. There he bought expensive clothes and jewels, and a big house with lots of servants. Night after night, he gave great feasts with delicious food and good wine for his new friends.

"He thought he was having a wonderful time and enjoyed his expensive lifestyle. But soon he had spent all his money. His new friends left him, and everything he had, even his fine clothes, was sold to pay his debts.

"He wandered the city streets, dressed in rags, begging for something to eat. But there had been bad harvests and there was a shortage of food; no one had any to spare and he had to go hungry.

"At last, he got work looking after a man's pigs in the fields. Sometimes he was so hungry, he was tempted to eat the pigs' food.

"One day, when he was watching the pigs, he thought, 'My father's servants always have plenty to eat while I'm nearly starving to death. I'll go home and beg my father to forgive me for what I've done. I'm not worthy to be called his son anymore, but I'll ask him to let me be one of his servants.'

"After a long, weary journey, the son reached his home, tired, dirty and wearing rags. While he was still some way from the house, his father saw him coming. He felt very sorry for his son, and ran to meet him. He threw his arms around his son and hugged him.

"'Forgive me, father. I've been very foolish,' said the son. 'I don't deserve to be your son anymore. Please let me be one of your servants.'

"The father took his son home. He told his servants to bring new clothes and shoes for his son. 'Tonight we'll have a feast; we'll eat and be merry. I thought my son was dead, but he is alive. I thought he was lost, but he has been found.'

"Out in the fields, the elder son heard the sound of laughter, music and dancing. He walked back to the house, and asked one of the servants what it was all about. 'Your brother has come home,' replied the servant. 'Your father is giving a feast with music and dancing because he is so pleased to see his son again.'

"The elder son was very angry and refused to go into the house. His father came out and asked him to come in. 'I've worked hard for you all these years. I've always done what you asked me, but you've never given me anything, not even a party for me and my friends,' shouted the son. 'But as soon as my brother comes home, having taken and wasted half your money, you order a great feast for him.'

"'My son,' said the father, 'you are always with me and everything I have is yours. Please try to understand. I thought your brother was lost or dead. Now I'm so happy and want to celebrate that he has come home, alive and well.'"

On the Road to Jericho

When Jesus and his disciples were walking to Jericho, a huge
crowd followed them, all talking and asking questions. Sitting by
the dusty road was a blind man, who couldn't work and each day
begged for food. When he heard the noisy people coming down the
road, he asked, "What's going on? What can you see?"

"It's Jesus," someone told him. "He's coming this way." The blind
man had heard of Jesus, and began to shout, "Jesus of Nazareth,
have pity on me." People told him to be quiet, but he only shouted
more loudly, again and again, "Jesus, have pity on me."

Jesus heard him and asked a disciple to bring the man to him.
When he came, Jesus said, "What do you want me to do for you?"
"I want you to make me able to see," answered the man. "So you
shall," said Jesus. "Your faith has done this for you." At once the
man regained his sight. Joyfully he joined the crowd around
Jesus, saying prayers of thanks to God.

A very rich tax collector from Jericho,
named Zacchaeus, wanted to see Jesus. He
was a small man and he couldn't see
Jesus because of all the people around
him. He ran ahead of the crowd and climbed
up a tree, knowing Jesus would come that way.

When Jesus walked under the tree, he looked up and
saw Zacchaeus sitting on the branches. "Zacchaeus,
come down," he said. "Take me to your house. I want to stay
with you." So they went to his house and Zacchaeus gave half
of all his possessions to the poor and offered to repay four times
over everyone whom he had made pay too much tax.

Jesus Rides into Jerusalem

Jesus and his disciples walked to the great city of Jerusalem.
Jesus wanted to be there for the special festival of the Passover.
On the way, they stopped near the village of Bethany.

Jesus said to two of his disciples, "Go into the village. There you
will find a donkey that has never been ridden. Untie it and bring it
here. If anyone asks you why you are taking it, tell him, 'The Lord
needs it and will return it,' and he will let you have it."

The two disciples did as Jesus told them, and found the donkey
tied by a door near a crossroads. When they untied it, they were
asked why they were taking it, and replied as Jesus had told them.
They led the donkey back to Jesus, and spread their cloaks over
its back to make a soft seat. Then Jesus got on the donkey, and
rode into Jerusalem with his disciples walking at his side.

When the crowds of people walking to the city saw Jesus coming,
they were very excited. Some spread their cloaks on the road in
front of the donkey's hoofs. Others cut down palm leaves to lay on
the road. They cheered and shouted, "Blessed is he who comes
in the name of the Lord. Praise be to God."

Jesus and his disciples went into the city and
walked through the streets to the Temple.
Then they left, and went back to the
village of Bethany for the night.

The next morning, Jesus went again to the Temple in Jerusalem to pray. The courtyard in front of the Temple was like a market, with traders selling cows, sheep and doves and changing money. Jesus was very angry. He stormed through it, overturning the tables of the money-changers and the seats of the traders, driving them, and the animals and birds out of the Temple courtyard.

"God's house is a house of prayer," he shouted, "but you have turned it into a den of thieves."

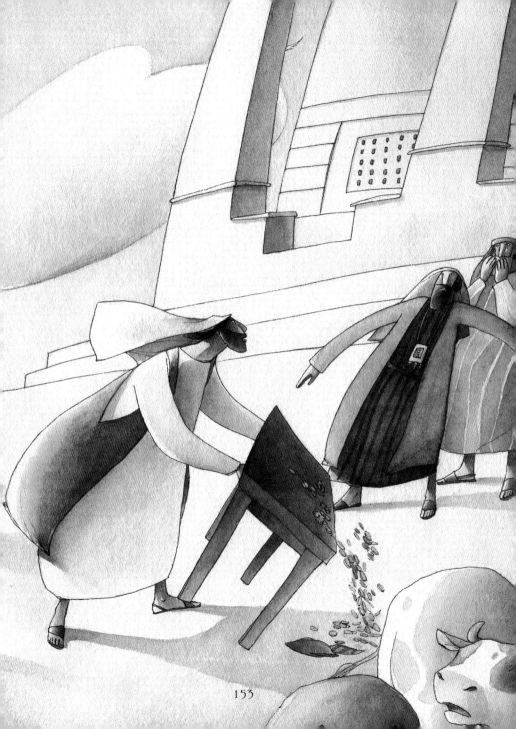

153

When all was quiet and peaceful again,
Jesus talked to the throngs of people, teaching them
about God, and healing the ones who were ill.

The chief priests and rulers of the Temple heard what Jesus had
done, and decided they must get rid of him. They were afraid of
him and the way the people flocked to hear him. They didn't dare
arrest him while he was in the Temple courtyard because they were
frightened that the people might riot to protect him.

They plotted to do it when there was no one to see them. Judas
Iscariot, one of the twelve disciples, went secretly to the chief
priests of the Temple. Now he was ready to betray Jesus.

"What will you give me if I tell you where and when you could
safely arrest Jesus," he asked the chief priests. They were
very pleased to see Judas and promised to give
him thirty silver coins.

From then on, Judas Iscariot waited and
watched for the right moment to betray Jesus
to the Temple priests. It had to be when he
was alone, with no crowds of people to
defend him.

The Last Supper

A few days before the Feast of the Passover, which reminded the Jews of when God freed them from being slaves in Egypt, the disciples asked Jesus where they would have this special meal.

"Go to Jerusalem," said Jesus to Peter and John. "There you'll meet a man carrying a jug of water. Follow him to his house. Ask the owner to show you a room where we'll have the Feast of the Passover together."

Peter and John went to Jerusalem, found the man with the water jug, and followed him to his house. There they made a room upstairs ready, and that evening Jesus and the other ten disciples arrived for the meal.

Before they sat down to eat, Jesus filled a basin with water, picked up a towel and knelt in front of each disciple, one by one, to wash their feet, drying them with the towel. This work was usually done by a servant and so when Jesus came to Peter, the disciple protested, "I can't let you wash my feet, Lord." Jesus replied, "If you won't let me wash your feet, then you can't be part of me."

When he had finished, Jesus sat down at the table with his disciples. "I, your Lord, have washed your feet, and you should wash one another's feet. I've set you an example to show that the Master is no more important than the servant, and that you should always behave humbly and kindly to each other."

Jesus talked to the disciples for a while and then he was silent. The disciples quietly watched him. They could see something was wrong because he looked so sad. Jesus knew he wouldn't be with them much longer, but would die soon.

At last, he said, "One of you will betray me." The disciples were stunned. They stared at each other in horror, wondering who it would be. Then one of the disciples, who was sitting next to Jesus, asked, "Which one of us is it, Lord?" "It is the one I give this bread to," answered Jesus.

He broke off a piece of bread from a loaf, dipped it in the sauce in a dish and handed it to Judas Iscariot. "Do what you have to do," he said. Judas Iscariot got up quickly from the table and slipped out of the room into the night.

When he had gone, Jesus told his disciples how much he loved them, but he would soon leave them. He told them that they would not be alone, that God would send his Spirit to help them, and that they were not to be afraid.

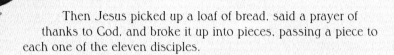

Then Jesus picked up a loaf of bread, said a prayer of thanks to God, and broke it up into pieces, passing a piece to each one of the eleven disciples.

"Eat this bread which is my body and remember me," he said. Then he picked up a cup of wine, said a prayer, and passed it to the disciples. "This is my blood which I give for you and for many people," he said. "Drink it and remember me."

When they had finished the supper, Jesus and his disciples sang a hymn and then went out into the dark streets. They walked to a garden of olive trees, called Gethsemane. On the way, Jesus told his disciples that they would soon run away and leave him alone.

"I would rather die than do that," loudly protested Peter. "I tell you that you will swear you don't know me three times before the cock crows at dawn tomorrow morning," Jesus said quietly to him.

At Gethsemane, Jesus asked some of his disciples to stay near the gates while he prayed to God. He walked on to a quiet place in the garden with Peter, James and John, and then went on alone to pray for the courage to face the terrible time that was coming.

When he went back to Peter, James and John, Jesus found they were fast asleep. "Couldn't you stay awake for just one hour?" he asked. "Please keep watch while I pray," and he walked away. After he had said his prayers, Jesus again went back to the three disciples and, again, he found they had gone to sleep.

The third time Jesus woke them up, they could hear loud voices and see torches flaring in the dark. It was the Chief Priests with the Temple guards. Judas Iscariot was leading them to where they could find Jesus and arrest him, far from any watching crowds.

Judas Iscariot walked up to Jesus and kissed him on the cheek. "This is the man you want," he said to the guards. When the guards stepped forward to take Jesus, Peter drew his sword and tried to defend him. He slashed off the ear of one of the High Priest's servants.

"Put away your sword," Jesus said to Peter and, touching the man's ear, made it whole again. Then he asked the High Priests, "Why have you come here with swords and clubs as if I were a criminal?" But they said nothing.

The disciples were very frightened. They ran away, just as Jesus said they would, leaving him alone. The guards grabbed Jesus roughly by the arms and marched him back to Jerusalem.

Sentenced to Die

Late that night, Jesus was taken by the Temple guards to the palace of Caiaphas, the High Priest. Many of the Jewish leaders were summoned there for the trial, although it was very late.

Peter secretly followed Jesus through the streets to the palace courtyard. As he stood with some of the guards, warming himself by their fire, a servant girl walked past and looked at him. "You were with Jesus of Nazareth," she said. "I don't know what you mean," answered Peter. A little while later, another servant said to him, "This man was with Jesus." "I don't know him," swore Peter.

As Peter stood talking to the guards, a man said, "You must know Jesus. I can tell you come from Galilee." Peter was very frightened. "I tell you, I don't know the man," he shouted. At that moment, a cock crowed three times and Peter remembered that Jesus had told him he would deny knowing him three times.

Peter was so appalled by what he had done, he ran out of the courtyard and hid in a dark corner, where he cried bitter tears of shame.

In the palace, the Chief Priests and the Jewish leaders began the trial of Jesus. They brought in many people who had been bribed to tell lies about Jesus, but their stories didn't match up. The leaders wanted to find an excuse to kill Jesus but, however hard they tried, they couldn't prove that he had done anything wrong. All through the trial, Jesus said nothing, and wouldn't answer any of the charges.

At last, the High Priest questioned Jesus. "Why won't you answer?" he asked, but Jesus didn't reply. Then the High Priest asked if he was the Son of God. "I am," replied Jesus, quietly. "You heard what the prisoner said," declared the High Priest to the people. "We don't need any more witnesses. He claims to be equal with God and that is blasphemy. Do you find him guilty or not guilty?" "Guilty," shouted the people, and they hit Jesus and spat at him.

The High Priest sentenced Jesus to death, but before he could have Jesus killed, he had to have permission from Pontius Pilate, the Roman Governor. Only the Roman Governor could give the order for an execution.

When Judas heard that Jesus was to die, he was bitterly sorry that he'd given Jesus away to the Chief Priests. He ran to the Temple. "I've betrayed an innocent man," he said and threw down the thirty silver coins they had given him. Then he went away and hanged himself.

163

The priests picked up the coins. "We can't put this money into the Temple treasury because it's linked to the death of Jesus; it's as if there was his blood on it," they said. After much discussion, they decided to buy a field to be used as a burial ground for foreigners. It became known as the Field of Blood.

In the morning, Jesus was taken to Pontius Pilate. The Chief Priests knew the Roman Governor wouldn't sentence a man to death for blasphemy against God, so they accused him of treason, a crime against Roman laws.

Jesus stood in front of the Roman Governor, who asked him, "Are you the King of the Jews?" Jesus replied, "It is as you say." When Pontius Pilate asked him other questions, Jesus wouldn't answer him and remained silent. In the end, the Roman Governor realized that Jesus was innocent of the charges but he didn't want to make the Jewish leaders angry by setting him free.

At that time, it was the custom for the Roman rulers of the country to set one prisoner free at the Feast of the Passover. The people could choose who it would be. Pontius Pilate asked the crowd if he should free Barabbas, who was a convicted murderer, or Jesus. The Chief Priests and the Jewish leaders persuaded the crowd to shout, "Free Barabbas! Free Barabbas!"

"What shall I do with Jesus?" Pontius Pilate asked the people. "Crucify him, crucify him," they shouted. "What harm has he done?" asked Pontius Pilate, but the crowd only shouted louder and louder, "Crucify him, crucify him."

The Roman Governor knew it was wrong to give in to them, but he was afraid they would riot. He called for a bowl of water and washed his hands, saying, "I'm not responsible for this man's death. It's your doing." Then he ordered that Barabbas should be released and Jesus should be flogged before being taken by the guards to be crucified.

The soldiers led Jesus away. They dressed him in a purple robe and pressed a crown made of thorns down on his head. They mockingly knelt in front of him and jeered, "Hail, King of the Jews." They beat him and spat at him. Then they dressed him in his own clothes, and dragged him away to be crucified.

Death on a Cross

The soldiers led Jesus through the streets of Jerusalem, making him carry a huge wooden cross. Jesus was very tired and weak from all the beatings he had been given, and he stumbled and fell again and again under the weight of the cross.

At last, a soldier made a man named Simon, who was standing in the street watching the procession, carry the cross for Jesus.

They struggled on to a place outside the city walls, called Golgotha. There the guards nailed Jesus to the cross by his hands and feet. They nailed a sign above his head which said, "Jesus of Nazareth, King of the Jews." Then they set up the cross between two other crosses. On them were thieves who had also been sentenced to death. Jesus looked down at the soldiers and the people watching. "Forgive them, Father," he prayed. "They don't know what they are doing."

Some of his enemies in the crowd shouted to him. "If you really are the Son of God, come down from the cross. Then we'll believe you," they taunted. The Chief Priests called out, "You saved others, why don't you save yourself?"

One of the thieves on a cross jeered at Jesus, saying, "If you really are the King of the Jews, save yourself and us." The other one answered, "We deserve to die but this man has done no wrong." Then he said to Jesus, "Remember me, Jesus, when you come as King." Jesus answered, "I tell you truly that today you'll be with me in paradise."

Mary, the mother of Jesus, was standing near the cross with John, one of the disciples. Jesus looked down at them. "Take care of her as if you were her son," he said to John and, from then on, John took care of Mary.

At noon, the sky grew strangely dark for about three hours. The crowd of people standing around the cross watched and waited in silence. At three o'clock, Jesus looked up and cried, "My God, why have you abandoned me?" Bowing his head, he said, "Father, I put my spirit into Your hands," and he died.

At that moment, the ground shook and the curtain in the Temple ripped from top to bottom. Many of the soldiers and the people were very frightened. One Roman soldier looked up at Jesus and said, "This man really was the Son of God."

The crowds drifted away to the city but Mary, the mother of Jesus, Mary Magdalene, Mary, the mother of the disciple James, and some of their other friends stayed by the cross. To make sure Jesus was dead, a soldier thrust a spear into his side. Then the soldiers took Jesus down from the cross.

Joseph, a rich man from Arimathea, who believed in Jesus, went to Pontius Pilate, the Roman Governor. He asked for permission to take Jesus away for burial. Pontius Pilate agreed and ordered that Joseph should be given the body.

Joseph carried the body away, accompanied by some friends of Jesus, and wrapped it in a linen cloth. Then they took it to a new tomb which had been cut into the rock on a hillside garden outside Jerusalem. They laid the body in the tomb. Then they rolled a huge, heavy stone in front of it, like a door, to close it. It was now Friday evening. The Jewish Sabbath begins at sunset, and they had to leave the proper burial of Jesus until the Sabbath on Saturday was over in the evening.

The Jewish leaders asked the Roman Governor to appoint a guard to watch the tomb. They were afraid that someone might try to steal the body and claim that Jesus had come alive again. Pontius Pilate gave the order; his soldiers put a seal on the tomb and stood guard over it during the night.

The Empty Tomb

Very early on Sunday morning, just before dawn,
Mary Magdalene and two friends went to the tomb to
finish the preparations for the burial. They wondered how
they would roll away the huge stone that blocked the entrance.

When the women reached the hillside, they were
astonished to see that the stone had been rolled
away from the tomb and the soldiers
guarding it had gone. A man in shining
white clothes told them, "Don't be
frightened. I know you are looking for
Jesus. He's not here. He is alive." When
the women looked into the tomb, they
saw it was empty; the body had gone.

Puzzled and a little frightened, the three women ran
to tell the disciples and friends of Jesus. "They've
taken the Lord away and we don't know where they've
laid him," cried Mary. The disciples didn't believe her;
they thought the women must have imagined it.

Peter and John ran to the tomb to see for themselves. John
arrived first but hesitated to go in. When Peter came, he went
straight in and saw that the tomb was empty, but the cloths that
Jesus had been wrapped in were lying there. Peter and John
didn't know if the body had been stolen, or if Jesus had really
come alive again. Puzzled and anxious, they went quietly home.

Mary Magdalene went back to the tomb by herself. While she knelt, weeping, outside the tomb, Jesus came and stood beside her. "Why are you weeping? Who are you looking for?" he asked. Mary didn't look up; she thought it must be a gardener speaking to her. "I'm weeping because they've taken my Lord away. Please tell me where he is," she begged.

"Mary," said Jesus. Mary looked up and saw it was Jesus. "My Lord," she cried. "Go and tell my friends you've seen me, and that soon I'll be with my Father in Heaven," said Jesus. Full of joy, Mary ran to tell the disciples that she had seen Jesus and that he had spoken to her.

On the Road to Emmaus

On that Sunday evening, Cleopas and Simon, both friends of Jesus, were walking along the road from Jerusalem to the village of Emmaus. As they walked slowly and sadly, they talked about Jesus. After a while, a man caught up with them. It was Jesus but they didn't recognize him and thought he was a stranger.

"Why are you so sad?" Jesus asked them. "Are you the only stranger in all of Jerusalem who doesn't know what has happened there over the last three days?" asked Cleopas. "Why, what has happened?" asked Jesus.

"We were talking about Jesus of Nazareth," said Simon. "He was a great teacher. We believed he was sent by God to save our people, but the Chief Priests and the Roman rulers accused him of breaking the laws of God and of the Romans. They condemned him to death, nailed him to a cross and now he's dead. That was last Friday, three days ago. When some women went to his tomb today, they found that his body had gone. They said that an angel had told them that Jesus is alive."

Jesus told them that the ancient prophets had foretold that all this would happen and explained it to Cleopas and Simon. When they reached Emmaus, it was late in the evening. Cleopas and Simon thought that the stranger was going to walk on, so they invited him to stay and have supper with them.

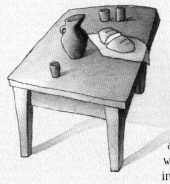

When they sat down to eat, the stranger picked up a loaf of bread. He broke it into pieces, said a prayer of thanks to God, and gave it to the two men. At that moment, Cleopas and Simon realized that the stranger was, in fact, Jesus. They stared at him in silence, and then he was gone.

Very excited, they talked about Jesus for a few minutes, and then decided they must go back to Jerusalem. Jumping up from the table, they ran all the way back to the city. Cleopas and Simon soon found some of the disciples and some other friends of Jesus. They told them that Jesus was alive, that they had seen him and spoken to him. At first, the disciples didn't believe them but one said, "It must be true. Peter has seen him too."

They locked
the door of the
room because
they were afraid of
the Roman rulers and
the Chief Priests. Then,
suddenly, Jesus was in the room
with them. "Peace be with you," he said. At first
they were very frightened; they thought he was a ghost.

"Don't be afraid," said Jesus. "Look at the wounds on my hands
and feet. Touch me and find out that I'm made of flesh and bone."
Then they knew that he really was Jesus.

"Have you anything to eat?" Jesus asked them. They gave him
some cooked fish and some honeycomb, and watched him eat it.
Jesus explained to them that this was all part of God's plan, and
that it had been foretold by the prophets.

"God's Son had to die and to come alive again on the third day,"
he said. "God forgives everyone who believes in me, His Son. This
is the message for all the people in the world, and you must go
and tell them this."

Breakfast by the Lake

Over the next few weeks, the disciples and friends of Jesus often saw and spoke to him. Peter and some other disciples left Jerusalem and went to Lake Galilee. One evening, Peter decided to go fishing. He set sail across the lake with some of the disciples. All night they threw their nets into the water, again and again, but each time they dragged them in, the nets were empty.

In the morning, when they were sailing back to the shore, they saw a man standing beside the lake. "Have you caught any fish?" he called. "No, nothing," they shouted back. "Throw your net over the right side of the ship," called the man. They did as he said and the net was so full of fish they couldn't pull it in.

One of the disciples said, "It must be Jesus." Peter immediately dived out of the boat into the water and swam to the shore. The other men rowed the boat to the beach, dragging in the net bulging with fish. Although it was very heavy, the net didn't break. Jesus had lit a fire and had cooked some fish over it.

"Come and eat, and bring some of the fish you've caught too,"
Jesus said, and he gave the disciples the cooked fish and some
bread. No one dared to ask the man who he was, but they all
knew it was Jesus.

When they had all eaten, Jesus looked at Peter, "Do you love me?" he asked. "Yes, Lord, you know everything. You know that I love you." Jesus again asked Peter the same question two more times, and each time Peter answered that he did love Jesus. And each time, Jesus said to him, "Take good care of my followers."

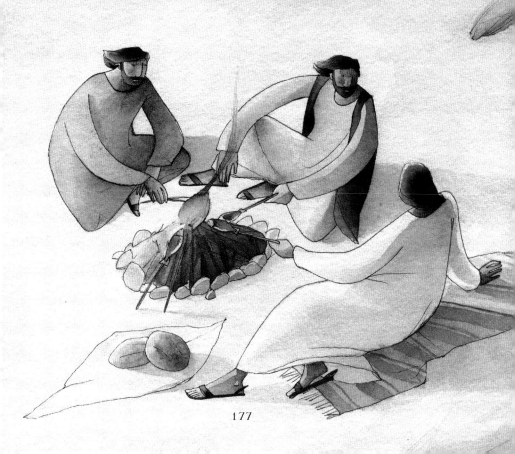

Wind and Fire

The last time his disciples saw Jesus was when they were walking
on the Mount of Olives outside Jerusalem. Jesus had come to say
goodbye. It was forty days since he had died and come alive again.

"You must go back to Jerusalem and wait there," Jesus told them.
"John baptized people with water but soon God will baptize you
with the Holy Spirit. He will give you the courage and power to
speak bravely to the people in Jerusalem, in Judea and Samaria,
and even in the whole world. Tell them the good news: that
everyone who trusts in me, and truly regrets the wrongs they have
done, will be forgiven. I will give each one of them a new life. And
remember, I shall always be with you."

When he had finished speaking, a cloud hid Jesus and he was
taken up into Heaven. As the disciples watched, they saw two men
appear, dressed in white. "You men of Galilee, why are you looking
up at Heaven? Jesus has gone to be with God but, one day, he will
come back," they said.

The disciples walked back to Jerusalem, feeling very happy, and
waited as Jesus had told them. On the day of the Jewish festival
of Pentecost, which celebrated the end of the wheat harvest, fifty
days after the Feast of the Passover, the disciples were in a house
in the city. Many other friends of Jesus, men and women, as well
as Mary, his mother, were also there.

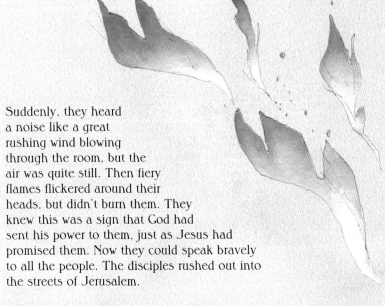

Suddenly, they heard
a noise like a great
rushing wind blowing
through the room, but the
air was quite still. Then fiery
flames flickered around their
heads, but didn't burn them. They
knew this was a sign that God had
sent his power to them, just as Jesus had
promised them. Now they could speak bravely
to all the people. The disciples rushed out into
the streets of Jerusalem.

The city was crowded with Jews who had come from as far
away places as Egypt, North Africa, Persia, Crete and Arabia for
the Feast of Pentecost. They were amazed when the disciples
spoke to them in their own languages, languages the disciples had
never learned or spoken before.

The disciples talked to them about God, and about Jesus and all
the wonderful things he had done. They told the people that they
should be baptized in the name of Jesus. They should regret the
wrongs they had done, and believe that Jesus had died for them
and they would be forgiven. They should begin new lives, knowing
that God would always help them and be with them.

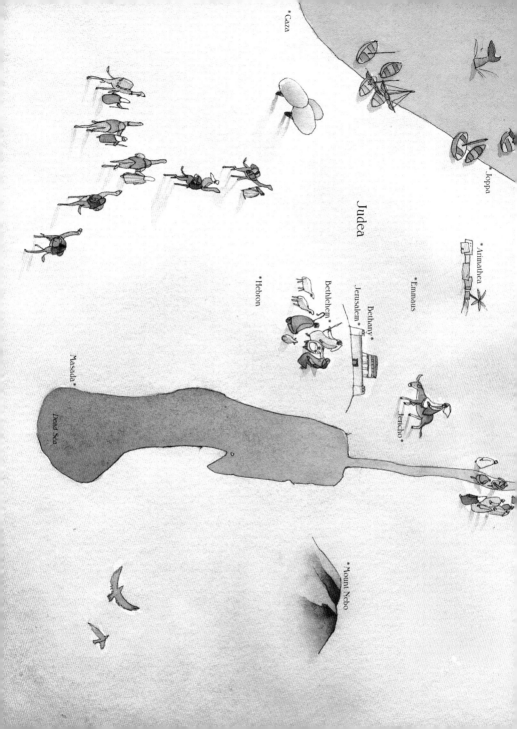

Who's who in the Bible

Aaron: the brother, companion and helper of Moses. He spoke to the King of Egypt on behalf of Moses, asking him to let the Hebrews leave Egypt.

Aaron

Absolom: son of David, who fought his father for the Kingdom.

Abraham: one of the main ancestors of the Jewish people; God made promises to him and his descendants so he was known as Father of the Jewish people. His son was Isaac.

Adam: the first man, created by God to live in the Garden of Eden.

Ahab: King of Israel who ruled at the time of the prophet, Elisha, and was married to Jezebel.

Andrew: one of the twelve disciples of Jesus; a fisherman and brother of Simon and Peter.

Artaxerxes: the King of Persia who allowed Nehemiah to return to Jerusalem, to help the Jews there obey the Laws of God.

Barabbas: a murderer who was freed instead of Jesus.

Bartholomew: one of the twelve disciples of Jesus.

Belshazzar: the King of Babylon who saw a ghostly hand write a warning on a wall during a feast.

Benjamin: the youngest of Jacob's twelve sons.

Boaz: the kind farmer who helped and married Ruth when she settled in Bethlehem with Naomi.

Caiaphas: the high priest in Jerusalem at the time of the trial and crucifixion of Jesus.

Cleopas: one of the men who met Jesus on the road to Emmaus, after Jesus had died on the cross.

Cyrus: the King of Babylon who let the captive Jews return to Jerusalem to rebuild the Temple there.

Daniel: a Hebrew boy who grew up in Babylon and held important positions under the kings. Faithful to God, he survived imprisonment, and a night in a pit of lions.

Darius: King of Babylon who had Daniel put into the lions' pit.

David: a shepherd boy who killed the giant Goliath with a stone. He became a great friend of King Saul's son, Jonathan, and grew up to become the King of Israel.

Delilah

Delilah: the Philistine woman who discovered the secret of Samson's great strength.

Disciples: friends and followers of Jesus; there were twelve special disciples, also known as apostles: Andrew, Peter, Philip, Simon, Bartholomew, Thomas, James, another James, Simon, Judas, Judas Iscariot and Matthew.

Ebedmelech: servant of King Zedekiah, who rescued Jeremiah from a muddy pit.

Elijah: a great prophet of Israel who constantly struggled to keep the people faithful to God and was often in danger from King Ahab, ruler of Israel, who prayed to the god Baal.

Elisha: the prophet who followed Elijah, and cured Naaman of his skin disease, and brought a widow's son back to life.

Elizabeth: the mother of John the Baptist, and cousin of Mary, the mother of Jesus.

Esau: the son of Isaac and Rebecca, whose twin brother, Jacob, tricked him out of his inheritance.

Esther: the young Jewish queen of the Persian King Xerxes. She saved her people from being killed.

Elijah

Eve: the first woman, whom God created. She lived with Adam in the Garden of Eden.

Goliath

Gabriel: the angel who told Mary that she would give birth to a son whose name would be Jesus.

Goliath: a giant Philistine soldier who was killed by David.

Hebrews: the name of the Jewish people, also called Israelites.

Herod the Great: the governor of Galilee and King of Judaea. He heard of the birth of Jesus from the Wise Men and tried to have him killed.

Herod Antipas: son of Herod the Great, he had John the Baptist put to death.

Herodias: the wife of Herod Antipas and mother of Salome.

Hiram: King of Tyre, who supplied Solomon with cedar wood for the building of the Temple.

Isaac: the son of Abraham and Sarah, husband of Rebecca and the father of Jacob and Esau.

Israel: the name given to Jacob whose sons fathered the twelve tribes of Israel. They later settled in the Promised Land; Israel is also the name of the kingdom.

Israelites: God's special people. They went to live in Israel, the Promised Land, and were also known as Hebrews and Jews.

Jacob: Isaac's son. He stole the inheritance from his twin brother, Esau and had twelve sons. He was also named Israel.

Jairus: the synagogue leader whose daughter Jesus brought back to life.

Jonah

James: the name of two of the twelve disciples of Jesus.

Jeremiah: a prophet who lived in Jerusalem; he was very unpopular as he foretold the destruction of the city by the Babylonians.

Jeroboam: an official in King Solomon's court. He became the first King of the ten Northern tribes when Israel split into two kingdoms under King Rehoboam.

Jesus: believed by Christians to be the Son of God; his life, teaching, miracles, death and resurrection are the subject of the New Testament.

Jews: God's special people. They were also known as Hebrews and Israelites.

John: one of the twelve disciples of Jesus.

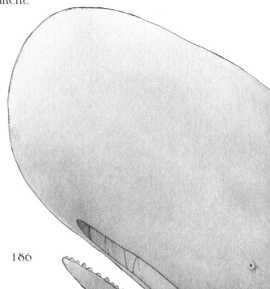

Joseph

John the Baptist: the cousin of Jesus. He told the people to be prepared for the coming of Jesus and was beheaded on the orders of King Herod Antipas.

Jonah: a reluctant prophet who was swallowed by a whale after he refused to obey God's orders.

Jonathan: the son of King Saul, and King David's great friend.

Joseph: Jacob's much-loved son who was sold as a slave and became a great ruler in Egypt.

Joseph: husband of Mary, the mother of Jesus.

Joseph of Arimathea: provided a tomb for Jesus.

Joshua: became leader of the Israelites after Moses, and captured the city of Jericho.

Judah: one of Jacob's twelve sons. His descendants were one of the twelve tribes of Israel. Judah was also the name of a kingdom.

Judas Iscariot: the disciple of Jesus who betrayed him to the chief priests and Temple guards, in return for thirty silver coins.

Laban: brother of Rebecca and father of Rachel.

Lazarus: brother of Mary and Martha, whom Jesus brought back to life after he had been dead for three days.

Lot: Abraham's nephew, who parted from
Abraham to take the best land for his flocks.

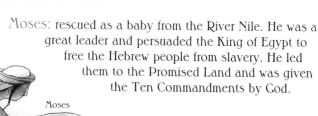

Mary

Manoah: father of Samson

Martha: a good friend of Jesus,
and sister of Mary and Lazarus.

Mary: the mother of Jesus.

Mary: sister of Martha and Lazarus,
and a good friend of Jesus.

Mary Magdalene: a friend of Jesus.
She was the first to see Jesus again
after his death.

Matthew: a tax collector who became
one of the twelve disciples of Jesus.

Meshach: friend of Daniel.

Michal: daughter of King Saul and wife of David.

Miriam: sister of Moses.

Moses: rescued as a baby from the River Nile. He was a
great leader and persuaded the King of Egypt to
free the Hebrew people from slavery. He led
them to the Promised Land and was given
the Ten Commandments by God.

Moses

188

Naaman: an army general. His skin disease was cured by Elisha.

Naboth: killed by King Ahab for his vineyard, after a plot by Queen Jezebel.

Naomi: mother-in-law of Ruth who returned to her home in Bethlehem.

Nebuchadnezzar: the powerful king of Babylon who captured Jerusalem, destroyed and looted Solomon's Temple, and took the Jewish people into exile.

Nehemiah: a Jewish exile in Babylon, he was allowed to return to Jerusalem by King Cyrus, to rebuild the city and the Temple.

Noah: a man faithful to God. He built an ark to save his family and all the animals from a great flood which God sent to drown the world.

Noah

Peter: a fisherman and one of the twelve disciples of Jesus.

Pharisees: members of a group of strict Jewish leaders who plotted against Jesus.

Philistines: people who were constantly at war with the Israelites, invading their borders.

Rebecca

Pontius Pilate: Roman governor of Judaea who ordered the death of Jesus.

Potiphar: captain of the Egyptian King's guard who bought Joseph as a slave.

Rachel: Jacob's best-loved wife, and mother of Joseph and Benjamin.

Rebecca: Isaac's wife, and mother of Jacob and Esau.

Ruth: daughter-in-law of Naomi. She went to Bethlehem with her.

Salome: daughter of Herodias who asked for the head of John the Baptist.

Samaritans: the inhabitants of Samaria, and the name of a separate Jewish sect. The Samaritans and Jews in Israel hated each other.

Samson: immensely strong Israelite who fought against the Philistines. They discovered the secret of his strength and captured him.

Sarah: Abraham's wife, and mother of Isaac.

Samson

Saul: first King of Israel. His son, Jonathan, was a great friend of King David. King Saul was killed by the Philistines.

Shadrach: one of Daniel's friends.

Simeon: one of Jacob's twelve sons.

Simon: one of the twelve disciples of Jesus.

Simon of Cyrene: the man who carried the cross for Jesus through the streets of Jerusalem.

Solomon: son of David and wise King of Israel, he built the Temple in Jerusalem.

Thomas: one of the twelve disciples of Jesus. He couldn't believe that Jesus had risen from the dead until he saw him for himself.

Zacchaeus

Vashti: the wife of King Xerxes.

Xerxes: the Persian King who married Esther.

Zacchaeus: the short tax collector who climbed a tree to see Jesus.

Zechariah: husband of Elizabeth, and father of John the Baptist.

Zedekiah: last King of Judah. He was captured by the Babylonians.

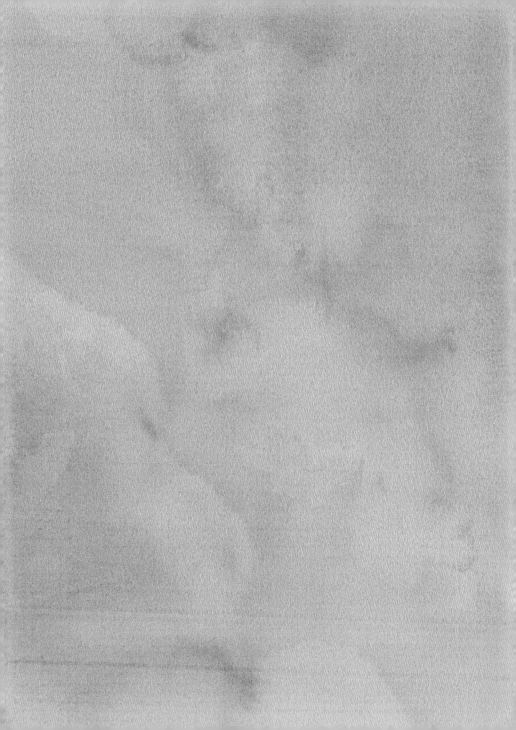